Praise for Geoff Symon

"Written with the perfect blend of information, sensitivity, and humor, Geoff Symon's "Autopsies" is a must-have research tool for any writer or anyone who simply wants the real story on what happens in the morgue. Real-life examples, illustrations, and do's/don'ts make this the most accessible, approachable research text I've encountered in my twenty years of writing crime fiction."
– Karen Rose, *New York Times*, *USA TODAY*, London's *Sunday Times*, Germany's *der Spiegel*, and the *Irish Times* bestselling author

"Whether it's crime scenes, sensational cases, or the ins and outs of autopsies—Geoff Symon is my go to guy. He makes learning about forensics both fascinating and fun. Everything he writes is an autobuy for me."
– Dee Davis, award winning, bestselling author

Autopsies

Forensics for Fiction Series

by Geoff Symon

Published by Evil Mastermind, LLC
New York, NY
EvilMastermind.com
First Publication: 1 December 2017

Edited by Tere Michaels
Illustrations by Evil Mastermind, LLC
Book formatting by BB eBooks

ISBN 978-1-945043-14-7 (Ebook)
ISBN 978-1-945043-15-4 (Print)

Website: www.ForensicsForFiction.com

To those who see death as an inspiration,
a story unearthed.

Contents

Acknowledgements   xi

Preface   xiii

Chapter 1: Introduction   1

    History   4

    Coroners vs. Medical Examiners   8

Chapter 2: Autopsy Basics   15

    The Body's Journey   16

    Forensic Autopsy   17

        Purposes of a Forensic Autopsy   18

        Remains Identification   28

        Final Medical Examinations   34

    Clinical Autopsy   35

    Psychological Autopsy   37

    Second Autopsy   39

    Reports   41

Case Study 1: Ryan Jenkins – Implanted Evidence   45

Chapter 3: The Autopsy – External Examination   53

    Vocabulary   54

    Personal Protective Equipment   57

    The Autopsy   57

    Intake   58

Radiology   62
Odontology   63
Anthropology   65
Entomology   67
External Examination   68

Chapter 4: The Autopsy – Internal Examination   71
Gaining Access   71
Organs   77
Head Dissection   88
Closing Up   94
Lab Work   96
Autopsy Report   99

Case Study 2: Beverley Allitt – False Angel   101

Chapter 5: Decomposition   111
Environmental Variables   112
Autolysis and Putrefaction   113
Saponification   118
Mummification   119
Bog Bodies   120
Skeletonization   121

Chapter 6: Time-of-Death Determinations   123
Witness Window   124
Decompositional Changes   125
Livor Mortis   126
Rigor Mortis   130
Algor Mortis   135
Potassium Release   138
Stomach Contents   139
Entomology   140

Chapter 7: Writing Your Autopsy   **145**

    The Body's Basic Interrogatory Menu   146

    Autopsy by Genre   151

    Considerations for Fictional Autopsies   158

       Spatial Awareness   159

       Bloody Mess   160

       Glamour Shots   160

       Tick Tock, Doc   161

       Come to Odor   161

       Bug Out   163

       Secret Identity   164

       No Body is Nobody   165

    Quick References   166

    Closing Thoughts   172

Glossary   175

Bibliography   193

Index   195

About the Author   201

Acknowledgements

To everyone who contributed and made this book a reality, I thank you. Specifically to Karen Rose, Lyla Bellatas, and Rayna Vause, whose time is precious and yet they spent it on me.

To Pamela Burford, who in the midst of making her life crazy, ironed the wrinkles out of mine, I thank you. Your sharp eye has been a draft-saver again and again.

A trumpet of praise rings out to Tere Michaels, who provided constant support along with her precise revisions. Anyone who can breathe life into a book about death is a master of her craft. Thank you.

And, of course, to my partner in crime, who finds the heartbeat in the projects I'm ready to pronounce dead.

Preface

When I taught forensics studies at the George Washington University in Washington, DC, and Marymount University in Maryland, I was amazed at my dedicated and enthusiastic students. As an adjunct professor, I first fully grasped how much interest exists for a career field to which I've dedicated twenty years.

I live with a successful author. Three years ago various writing groups and conventions began inviting me to present forensic courses at their gatherings. Authors turned out to be even hungrier for realism than I'd expected. They might deal in make-believe, but they wanted their stories anchored in truth.

All the different writer audiences made one thing clear: few reference books hit the sweet spot between minutiae and fluff. While many books exist on crimes and investigative techniques, very few address the unique challenges of writing genre fiction.

That need gave birth to the *Forensics for Fiction Series*. In these books, I'm distilling all of my training and experience as a twenty-year forensic investigator and my personal involvement with the genre community. Each book will provide a targeted overview of a different aspect of criminal investigations. I'll present each topic as a heaping platter of research goodies for writers of every genre to choose from, depending on what works for the story in front of them.

I want this book to be accessible and helpful, so rather than bury you under a wall of impenetrable text, I've broken up each chapter with insets:

- *PROCEDURES* and *TERMS*: highlighting how real-life law enforcement officials operate and actual language they use.
- *ACCURACY* and *PITFALLS*: providing practical tips to steer authors away from common errors.
- *FUN FACTS*: sharing entertaining tidbits to spark an idea or inspire a plot bunny.
- *ALERTS*: identifying specialized sections that may only interest exhaustive researchers. Whenever you see the Alert symbol—

—I am letting you know that the following section may be more technical than your book requires. If you don't need to know the physics and math involved, feel free to skip these marked sections. You can pick up at the next section seamlessly.

I make sure to provide plenty of illustrations to clarify and drive home every concept. Additionally, I include true-crime case studies relevant to the topic and talk about my own investigations.

I hope you find this book informative and entertaining, but mostly hope you find it useful in your next great story.

Chapter 1: Introduction

"Hic locus est ubi mors gaudet
succurrere vitae."
(This is the place where death delights
in helping the living.)
– Giovanni Battista Morgagni

We find the above Latin proverb on plaques in morgues across the globe. It serves as a reminder why the dissection of a human being is not merely a morbid task, but a valuable, often critical, step in discovering disease and identifying genetic disorders for surviving family members, as well as providing evidentiary contributions to criminal investigations. What many people see as macabre is actually an honorable and beneficial service.

Popular fiction is chock-full of post-death thrills. Agatha Christie uses the evidence found through the evaluation of bodies in many of her cozy mysteries, such as in *Murder on the Orient Express*. Patricia Cornwell uses autopsies to involve her protagonist, Dr. Kay Scarpetta, a medical examiner, in her series of crime thrillers. And let's not forget our classic paranormal stories rich in undead specialties. Vampires, such as Bram Stoker's *Dracula*, are forever kept in the freshest stages of decomposition, while zombies (moist) and mummies (dry) exhibit opposite spectrums of extreme decay. While in Mary Shelley's tale, Dr. Frankenstein had to examine the compatibility of body parts as he exhumed corpse after corpse to build his monster.

Autopsies: Forensics for Fiction pulls back the curtain on forensic pathology to allow authors to see what actually happens to a body after death, both naturally and procedurally, and explains how an autopsy is conducted, revealing both what it tells us and what it cannot. I'll expose you to the terminology, which is heavy in Latin and Greek, and walk you through each step of the process to anchor your writing in credible specifics.

> **TERMS –** Forensic pathology is the branch of medicine tasked with determining how and why a person died, done through the dissection of that body.

When talking about medical procedures, much of this material may become overly technical and could exceed your needs for a simple scene in your story. I hope to keep this topic accessible and fun (yes, I said it) and engaging for everyone, even those who may have merely picked up this book due to an (understandable) morbid curiosity. Welcome to my lair!

The term *autopsy* comes from Greek and literally means "to see for oneself." In modern English, it is the word we use for the dissection of a human body.

> **FUN FACT** – The terms "autopsy" and "necropsy" mean the same thing in modern English: the dissection of a corpse. However, autopsy is used when referring to a human body, while necropsy is typically used for an animal dissection.

The purpose of an autopsy is manifold: to determine why a person died and to identify the remains, as well as the lesser-known goal of learning about the person's pre-death health. Think of an autopsy as the very last medical examination this person will ever receive. The doctor performing the autopsy (called the **pathologist**) needs to go further than documenting a bullet's trajectory through the body. She needs to determine there are not any genetic ailments or contagious diseases that might threaten other family members, that may become a concern to society at large, or that may have even contributed to the person's death.

The type of pathologist who performs an autopsy, often either a coroner or medical examiner, varies from country to country, and typically also depends on whether the situation involves a death that is suspicious. England, Wales, Northern Ireland, and Ireland all have a coroner system. The United States and Canada have a mixture of a coroner and a medical examiner system. Japan has special units made up of police detectives, and Scotland gives the responsibility of autopsies for suspicious deaths to the sheriff.

As my expertise and experience fall solely within the United States concerning this topic, in this text I will focus primarily on the US structure and will cover both the coroner and medical examiner systems. If you are writing about an autopsy that occurs in a country other than the US, I urge you to research that nation's policies and practices, keeping in mind such factors as religious and cultural limitations.

🚨 ALERT – The following section becomes more technical than most writers need for their stories. It covers the history of autopsies, especially the development of the coroner system in England. Those not interested in the historical context of the US systems can skip ahead to the next section titled "Coroners vs Medical Examiners."

History

On any topic, I always feel we should understand the history behind it. Not only can such research give us handy cocktail-party-worthy tidbits, but it shows us the course and reasons for the subject's evolution. In this case, by learning how each program developed, you'll see the logic behind them, making it clearer why the US started with a pure coroner system, and why it's slowly converting into a medical examiner setup.

The origins of dissecting bodies date back to our earliest recorded history. Archaeological excavations revealed the ancient Egyptians removed organs in their embalming process, which we call mummification. In the Bible, Genesis 50:2, 3, and 26 refers to both Jacob and his son, Joseph, as being embalmed. Then, around 290 BCE, after Alexander the Great opened the Great Library of Alexandria in order to further scientific research and study, two physicians, Herophilus and Erasistratus, independently migrated to Alexandria. Later branded by Christians as "butchers," these doctors are credited with prominent advances in the understanding of human anatomy through their dissection of bodies.

The first known dissection for medicolegal purposes, which is to say in order to determine a cause of death as opposed to merely for religious beliefs or for scientific advancement, happened at the University of Bologna in Italy in 1302. The autopsy was ordered by the magistrate to decide whether there was any fault in the person's death, and required that a physician and a surgeon examine the body.

> **TERMS – Medicolegal is a term that pertains to procedural areas where the specialties of medicine, law, and law enforcement overlap.**

About this same time, the crowners, a special position established under the English monarchy, eventually developed routine medicolegal responsibilities. These medicolegal duties were not the office's original purpose.

Back in 1194, Richard the Lionheart (of Robin Hood fame) was King of England, but lived in France. He gave Hubert Walter sole reign of England and promoted him to Archbishop of Canterbury. England's reserves were mostly depleted due to King Richard's extravagant spending and a massive ransom paid to free him after he was captured by the Mayor of Vienna during one of his Crusades. Adding to the financial issues, the Crown was not receiving the payments seized by the local sheriffs when they imposed fines or collected taxes in their counties. The sheriffs were notoriously corrupt and kept the money for themselves. As the county's sole law enforcement entity, no one policed the sheriffs.

Desperate to raise money, Walter created a new office called the "crowner," what we now know as the "coroner." The crowners were set up as groups of three knights and one local civilian who traveled the countryside enforcing the interests of the Crown. Their duties were vast, ranging from tax collection to law enforcement to judicial resolutions.

Eventually, one of their duties became looking into local deaths as a means of generating income through fines. The crowners reviewed a person's death in its entirety, from what caused the death, to who reported finding the body, to how the body was handled afterwards. If they found anyone acting outside the overly complicated set of laws regarding these matters – regardless of whether their target was a witness, a doctor, a family member, or someone directly involved with the death itself – they issued massive fines that they would send back to the Crown.

> **FUN FACT** – The term "coroner" comes from the English word "crowner," who was a person appointed by the King and responsible for representing him on duties he decreed.

These death inquiries eventually became more focused on actual death investigations, i.e., determining how the person died. This new direction came about again as a means of confiscating money. If the crowners decided the death was a homicide, the Crown seized all of the offender's property. Likewise, if the death was ruled to be a suicide, the Crown seized all of the decedent's property. So, in order to gain money, it behooved the Crown to use the crowners to establish what type of death had occurred.

Eventually, as the need for the crowners diminished, their responsibilities were stripped away until they were solely responsible for the assessment of cause of death. Also, as time went on, the crowners eventually became simply locally appointed gentlemen. The Crown reasoned that a gentleman had no need for extra money because he was already successful, and therefore he was less likely to embezzle the money he seized. In this tradition, coroners are still locally elected officials today, and their primary responsibility is to investigate suspicious deaths.

When England colonized America, they brought their coroner system with them. The US solely used the coroner system until 1917, when New York City voted to abolish their Office of Coroner, which was facing allegations of severe incompetence as well as fraud, waste, and abuse of the authorities of the office. On January 1, 1918, New York City established the first Office of Chief Medical Examiner of the City of New York, a hired position on qualifications as opposed to being elected like a coroner. Since then, many states and even some other countries have established their own medical examiner's offices.

Coroners vs. Medical Examiners

One of the many questions I get from authors about autopsies is the most basic: Who performs them? Coroners? Medical examiners? Doctors? Elected officials? For the US, the answer to each of these is, "Yes."

In the US, each state determines their own system,

so across the country there are some states that use only coroners, some that utilize just medical examiners, and others that have a combination of the two systems. I spell out which system every state uses in a chart located in the Quick Reference section of Chapter 7. Make sure to know the correct system for the country, state, county, or district you're writing about.

How significantly do the coroner and medical examiner systems differ? Let's first address how they are the same:

- Both offices are responsible for the medicolegal investigation of death. In other words, they both look into any death suspicious in nature.
- Both offices are limited to a geographical jurisdiction.
- Both offices may conduct death scene investigations.
- Both offices perform autopsies to determine a cause and manner of death.
- Both offices produce a report accessible by law enforcement and judicial authorities.

> **TERMS** – Suspicious death include those that are unattended (outside a doctor's care), unusual, sudden, unexplained, violent, or unnatural.

In coroner states, the system is county or district-based, meaning every county has its own coroner. The coroner is an official elected for a four-year term whose qualifications are solely up to the voting populace. This means some coroners must only meet the basic requirements needed to be on a ballot and do not necessarily have to be forensically trained or even be doctors. To be clear, some coroner states do require qualifications such as a medical degree, but that is on a state-by-state basis. In those counties where the coroner is not a doctor, typically a deputy coroner is hired with those qualifications.

I should point out here, however, that not all doctors are forensic pathologists. Having a medical degree is not sufficient training to conduct a forensic examination of human remains. As we'll discuss in the next chapter, there is a difference between a hospital autopsy and a forensic autopsy. The point to take away from this is although there are extremely qualified coroners who are properly trained and able to perform a forensic autopsy, a significant degree of variability exists throughout the entire US coroner system.

> **TERMS** – Coroners are county-based elected officials responsible for the medicolegal investigations of suspicious deaths.

As stated above, in coroner systems, the coroner is specifically responsible for performing death inquiries. This does not mean they interview witnesses or process crime scene evidence. Law enforcement agencies still take care of the investigation. The coroner is in charge of all things that have to do with the body, which includes anything on-site at the crime scene. On-scene investigators cannot touch the body. They must wait for the coroner or deputy coroner to arrive at the scene, officially declare the person dead, and remove the remains. This means the decision whether or not to even conduct an inquiry or perform an autopsy is up to the coroner.

> ACCURACY – Law enforcement cannot touch a body at a crime scene for any reason, even to collect evidence. This is because a doctor needs to declare a body dead. The investigator cannot risk a situation where the body was not dead and his actions actually made the injuries worse. He can collect any evidence at the morgue.

When the coroner approves an autopsy, he must then also arrange for its location, decide who will perform it, and provide all equipment needed for its proper execution. In more rural counties, each of these logistical necessities becomes difficult.

The coroner is also responsible for issuing a death certificate. This becomes problematic when the elected official is not a licensed physician, as a doctor is required for death certification. In these situations the coroner typically must wait to sign the death certificate until the attending doctor pronounces the death.

Since New York City's switch in 1918, many local governments across the US have decided the coroner system is not adequate to perform its required duties. These opponents argue that elected officials are not only potentially unqualified, but waste taxpayers' money by having to hire additional personnel who are. They also opine that further money is wasted by hiring local rural pathologists on a case-by-case basis and sending equipment around the county. A third argument revolves around the inability of non-licensed coroners to certify the cause of death for the death certificate, which they must sign. Thus the medical examiner system came into existence.

A medical examiner is typically hired by the local government based on strict occupational require-ments. The medical examiner is a board-certified forensic pathologist. The medical examiner's office is usually set up to be self-contained for the entirety of death investigations. The office normally includes a staff of forensic pathologists who are ready to respond to scenes and perform autopsies, and laboratories to perform forensic analysis such as toxicology (drug/toxin tests), histology (microscopic evaluation), and, in some cases, DNA analysis. Some offices even have in-house investigators who act as liaisons with the local law enforcement agencies.

Like coroners, medical examiners are responsible for investigating suspicious deaths, determining a cause and manner of death, and providing a report to include a certificate of death. Unlike coroners, however, most medical examiners complete their duties in-house. Under a medical examiner system, law enforcement still cannot touch a body at a crime scene. The medical examiner's office responds to the scene, declares the person dead, and transports the remains back to their offices.

> **TERMS – Medical examiners are board-certified forensic pathologists hired to conduct medicolegal investigations of suspicious deaths.**

Every mile of the United States is covered by a coroner or medical examiner, but there are several areas where the jurisdiction is not so cleanly defined, specifically on Indian reservations.

Typically, everything that happens on an American Indian reservation is left to that reservation's local government to address. The state and federal government, except in specified situations, stay out of their society. Suspicious deaths can fall under the exceptions. The determination is made by the Bureau of Indian Affairs, a US government agency. If the BIA gives the body to the local coroner or medical examiner, as with all other cases, she has full control of the autopsy and makes all decisions on what is or is not done. This has resulted in many court cases by local Indian reservations who claim their religion is not honored by certain autopsy procedures or when they are not allowed to be physically near the body for several days, as their customs dictate. It is an extremely sensitive situation that has no clear ruling.

Once the coroner or medical examiner takes possession of any body, the autopsy process begins, although that typically includes storing the remains overnight. Before we get into the actual practice, I want to lay the groundwork with some preliminary information, which I'll discuss in the next chapter.

Chapter 2: Autopsy Basics

Before we get into autopsy procedures, I feel it's best to cover some basics about the autopsies themselves. Why do we do autopsies? Are there different types? What is expected afterward? Let's secure your footing before unearthing the good stuff.

First, I need to address a bit of vocabulary to avoid any confusion. The word *postmortem* is a Latin phrase that literally means "after death." In the forensics world, professionals use it regularly in a variety of ways. As an adjective and adverb, it conveys its true meaning. So, "a postmortem wound" means an injury that occurred after the person died. Likewise, "the body was moved postmortem" means that activity happened after the death.

However, when used as a noun, *postmortem* becomes synonymous with *autopsy*. In this instance, "the pathologist began the autopsy at 0900 hours," and "the pathologist began the postmortem at 0900 hours," are equally correct and are used interchangeably throughout the forensics community. I will cover several other medical terms over the next several chapters.

> **TERMS** – As a noun, "postmortem" and "autopsy" may be used interchangeably.

The Body's Journey

If a body is slated for autopsy, where does it go, and when does the family gain custody? There are several stops the body makes before burial. The site where the body is discovered is called the **death scene**. This can range from the hospital bed where a patient died, to the room where a loved one was found, to a crime scene where a victim was killed.

Depending on the type of autopsy – described below – the attending doctor will have the body delivered to the autopsy suite, known as the **morgue**. Morgues are found in hospitals, coroner/ME offices, and in any other medical facility, public or private, that conducts autopsies.

After the autopsy, the pathologist releases the remains to a mortician, who prepares the body for the funeral home. The mortician works in a **mortuary** and is responsible for embalming the body for burial or making arrangements for cremation, which requires a certified crematorium. Mortuaries are located outside of the medical facilities or coroner/ME office. They are often private, certified businesses. Today, most funeral home directors are themselves morticians, with the mortuary located at their funeral home.

The next of kin has access to the remains once they are housed at the funeral home.

TERMS – While a morgue and mortuary are often used interchangeably as a place that houses dead bodies in casual conversation, in the profession, a morgue is where the autopsy is conducted by a pathologist, while a mortuary is where the remains are prepared for burial or cremation by the mortician.

One important note about morticians and funeral home directors: All morticians must be certified to perform mortuary functions. As mentioned, many funeral home directors have gone through the certification process and are themselves morticians. The regulation of funeral homes and their directors, conversely, vary state to state. Many states have no standards that funeral homes must meet, while other states require their own in-state certification and oversight.

At the beginning of the body's journey, the coroner, medical examiner, or attending physician (if an attended, natural death) decide if there should be an autopsy. There are several types of autopsies, each performed for specific purposes:

- Forensic autopsy
- Clinical autopsy
- Psychological autopsy
- Second autopsy

Forensic Autopsy

When most authors write about autopsies, they are

referring to the **forensic autopsy**, also known as the **medicolegal autopsy**, which is part of a routine inquest. This procedure is done for any unnatural, unattended death. These are the autopsies conducted when the conditions of the death seem questionable or suspicious, and are the ones written about in crime stories.

> **TERMS – A forensic/medicolegal autopsy is conducted in unexplained, suspicious, or criminal deaths.**

The coroner/medical examiner has the authority to order a forensic autopsy based upon the review of the circumstances, in order to establish the *cause and manner of death*, which I'll address below. The next of kin are <u>not</u> a part of this authorization process and may <u>not</u> deny or limit the scope of this type of autopsy.

Ideally, these autopsies are conducted by a forensic pathologist, who is a doctor specifically trained via residency in forensic evaluation. The forensic pathologist's job is to determine the cause and manner of death, identify the deceased, preserve potential evidence for law enforcement investigations, and collect biological samples for further review.

Purposes of a Forensic Autopsy

As I touched on in the last chapter as an introduction, there are three primary reasons to conduct a forensic autopsy:

- To determine why a person died.
- To identify the remains.
- To provide a final, thorough medical examination for that person.

Let's delve into each of these objectives.

Death Determinations

Most crime dramas use the phrase "cause and manner of death" a lot, and it's an accurate representation of its actual use in my line of work. When professionals say "the cause and manner of death," what they are referring to is why the person died. How did he die? What was the series of events that resulted in death? However, to be completely accurate, a third descriptor, "mechanism of death," should be included in that list. Together, these three descriptors explain exactly what happened.

Death Determinations – Manner

The **manner of death** is a broad categorization of the circumstances, based on the pathologist's expert opinion. It explains what *kind* of death occurred. The pathologist has only five categories to choose from, and makes her determination based not only on the autopsy findings, but also on the details of the scene where the body was found and any other related information provided to her staff primarily from, but not solely limited to, law enforcement. The five manners of death are:

- Natural
- Accidental
- Homicide
- Suicide
- Undetermined

A <u>natural death</u> is one that occurred independent of external influences. Illness and biological defects are often the cause of natural deaths.

Some argue that certain natural deaths <u>are</u> a direct result of outside influence, such as a heart attack brought about by over-stressing the body, or cirrhosis caused by a lifetime of overdrinking. But these examples are simply of the body failing and are not considered homicide, suicide, or accidental. Even if the death is seen as tragic, such as an infant with an underdeveloped heart, the manner of death is still ruled as natural.

<u>Accidental deaths</u> are, as the name suggests, caused by accidents. They are deaths that occurred when, although there may have been an assumption of risk, death was not intentional.

A <u>homicide</u> is any death caused by another person. There is an important distinction to be made with this term, though. Homicide is a *medical term* and does not mean the death is *criminal* in nature. Crime is determined in the legal arena. For example, the crimes of murder and manslaughter are homicides; they are the illegal killing of one person by another.

Killing in self-defense is not a crime, yet it is also a homicide.

> **PITFALL –** Be careful in your stories not to have a pathologist's ruling of homicide mean anything more than a manner of death. To imply that a homicide means the suspect is guilty of a crime is a misuse of the term.

A suicide is any death intentionally brought on by the decedent himself.

The manner of undetermined is used when the death cannot be adequately placed in any of the other categories.

In an early case in my career, I investigated the death of a bodybuilder who was found in his bed with a rag on his face and a plastic bag over his head. The search of the death scene revealed an overabundance of steroids. The rag was tested and found to have an anesthesia on it called halothane. There just wasn't enough evidence at the scene or autopsy to determine whether this manner of death was homicide (someone knocked the deceased out with halothane and then suffocated him with the bag), suicide (the deceased knocked himself out after putting the bag on his head with the intention of killing himself), or accidental (the deceased used halothane to put himself to sleep because the steroids caused insomnia, but he needed the plastic bag to get the strongest hit of halothane as he built a tolerance to it). In cases such as these, where the death could apply to more than one category, the manner must be listed as undetermined.

Do all pathologists always agree with one another's manner of death determinations? No. Pathologists can get the manner of death wrong, and in some cases, especially in those where further information is developed after the autopsy report is published, the manner can be changed. It is not an easy process and does not happen often, but it is possible to change a manner of death.

In the Casey Anthony investigation, Dr. Jan Garavaglia ("Dr. G" of TV fame) was the attending medical examiner and made a manner of death determination for Caylee Anthony as homicide.

Dr. G was not able to gain scientific data from the autopsy. The bones were too decomposed and dry. There was no tissue to test. She based her ruling on the nonmedical evidence from the scene.

She opined that a missing child that wasn't reported for over a month, whose body was found in a garbage bag, discarded in a swamp, with duct tape near the face, was enough to preclude any other manner. She concluded the circumstances did not support a natural death, a suicide, or an accident. And as a forensic pathologist and expert in her field, she was allowed to take all of that information into account.

The defense in this trial, however, brought in another well-known forensic pathologist, Dr. Werner Spitz, who disagreed with Dr. G's ruling. He felt there was not enough medical data to make any manner of death determination.

Since homicide is not a legal determination, but a medical term, this disagreement should not have mattered. Dr. Spitz's opinion simply meant he, himself, needed more information to have confidence in any manner of death other than undetermined.

Neither of the pathologists were wrong, as the manner of death *is* an opinion reached by the attending pathologist. It's no different than one person saying he feels better because of chicken noodle soup and another saying she thinks he feels better because the flu has just run its course. Does either opinion really matter? No, the issue is the cold is gone. Likewise, having the manner classified as homicide or undetermined should have little effect on the case as a whole. A little girl is still dead.

However, the defense in this case presented the opposing views as greatly significant, implying the difference of opinion was actually a difference in scientific fact. Instead of recognizing that both were valid, he labeled the variance as "faulty forensics" to the jury, thus allowing him to paint any other testimony from Dr. G as suspect or "faulty" as well.

The manner of death is recorded on both the autopsy report and death certificate, in cases where a forensic autopsy was done. Sometimes the death certificate is published before the criminal investigation is complete, and some pathologists prefer to have all of the case's information before committing to a final manner. To avoid situations like that noted above in the Casey Anthony case, some death certificates include a sixth "manner." I use quotation marks because it is not a manner at all. On those certificates the pathologist has the option to choose "pending" as the manner, which simply means the final determination has not been made. "Pending" cannot be used as an easy out, however, and eventually must be changed to one of the five manner categories.

Death Determinations – Cause

The **cause of death** is the identification of the actions, events, or circumstances that directly led to the person dying: the disease or injury that resulted in the loss of life. A gunshot wound is a cause of death: the firing of the gun led to a bullet wound that led to death. Heart disease is another cause of death, as is appendicitis, electrocution, and blunt force trauma (from a car accident, for example).

The cause and manner of death are separate and distinct determinations. Depending on the circumstances, a cause of death, such as a gunshot wound, could have a manner of homicide (if the deceased was shot by someone else), suicide (if the deceased shot himself, intending to die), accidental (if there was an accidental discharge), or undetermined (if there's not enough evidence to place the case in any of the other categories). Obviously a gunshot wound can never be considered natural, but the point remains that the same cause of death can have very different manners of death. The example I gave above about my investigation into the bodybuilder's death is another instance where the cause of death – suffocation – could have different manners of death depending on the circumstances.

> **PITFALL** – When writing about a death in a story, do not blend the cause and manner of death. To write, "the cause of death was natural" is incorrect and inconsistent with what professionals actually say. These determinations are independent of each other. The manner of death is natural. The cause of death is heart disease.

The cause of death is annotated on all death certificates, regardless of whether there was a forensic autopsy. It is also the ultimate finding on autopsy reports.

Death Determinations – Mechanism

The **mechanism of death** is the physiological failure that resulted in the death. It is the *literal* reason the person died. If the manner of death is *what* type of death it was, and the cause of death is *why* the person died, then the mechanism is *how* he actually died.

So, let's return to our gunshot wound example. The gunshot wound is the cause of death because it is why the person died; it is the event that led to death. But the actual, literal reason the person died was loss of blood, medically referred to as exsanguination. Why did he die? Gunshot wound. How did he die? Exsanguination.

In the bodybuilder's case, while the cause of death is suffocation (asphyxiation), the mechanism of death is hypoxia, a fatally low level of oxygen in the blood that is available for the organs, in this case the brain.

Cardiac arrest (the heart stopped), loss of brain function, and kidney failure are all examples of mechanisms of death. They are all the cessation of a vital biological process.

The mechanism of death is described in the doctor's analysis in the autopsy report, but is not necessarily reported on the death certificate.

So when you write about the cause and manner of death, recognize their differences, and remember to keep the mechanism of death in mind as well.

- MANNER OF DEATH – One of five categories to which the death is assigned. (WHAT)
- CAUSE OF DEATH – The event that directly led to the death. (WHY)
- MECHANISM OF DEATH – The physiological failure that resulted in death. (HOW)

Diagnosis of Exclusion

I feel it is important to point out in our discussion of cause and mechanism of death that sometimes a doctor does not know why a person died. She does not know the cause and is not sure of the mechanism. If a cause or mechanism of death is ever described as "respiratory and cardiac arrest," that simply means the person stopped breathing and their heart stopped. But this happens in 100% of all deaths.

> **ACCURACY –** Cardiac arrest, which means the heart stopped, is a throwaway diagnosis. It happens in every single death.

There are certain situations where the doctor's conclusion is a **diagnosis of exclusion**, which, through the process of elimination, excludes every other possibility but really means the doctor does not know. A diagnosis of exclusion cannot be proven, it's what's left after everything else is *disproven*. Therefore, all tests must be performed and a thorough head-to-toe analysis must be conducted. Everything else must be excluded, i.e., shown not to be the cause of death, for a diagnosis of exclusion to be valid.

> **TERMS –** A diagnosis of exclusion is a conclusion for a cause of death that results from the elimination of every other possibility. It is what's left.

One such diagnosis of exclusion is Sudden Infant Death Syndrome, SIDS. The only way a pathologist can diagnosis a death as SIDS is if she has done a thorough autopsy and no cause of death is apparent. If she only conducted a partial autopsy, or if not all of the tests were conducted, then a diagnosis of SIDS should not be made. SIDS, at its most basic, simply means we don't know why the baby died, thus making it a diagnosis of exclusion.

> ACCURACY – It is incorrect to say a baby died <u>from</u> SIDS, as SIDS simply means no other cause of death is apparent. SIDS is not a diagnosis but an "I don't know" conclusion.

Remains Identification

If the above death determinations answer the *what*, *why*, and *how* of the death, what covers the rest of the basic interrogatory questions?

The *where* is determined through the investigation: where the body was discovered and, if different, where the death actually occurred. The *when* is a big part of the forensic autopsy, and I've given it its own chapter later in this book, titled Time-of-Death Determinations. That leaves us with the *who*, which, as we covered earlier, is one of the essential objectives of the forensic autopsy.

In September 2001, while with the Office of the Armed Forces Medical Examiner, I participated in the autopsies of the 9/11 deaths from the Pentagon and

Pennsylvania. In that case we already knew the cause of death: blunt force trauma, be it directly from the airplane crash, or debris from either the plane or building colliding with the bodies. So the *why* of the deaths was not the primary purpose of these autopsies. We conducted the autopsies to determine the *who*.

We needed to positively identify all of the bodies so that we could give the next of kin complete and accurate remains of their loved ones. Keep in mind that in this case not all of the bodies were in pristine, whole conditions. Many remains consisted of parts and often those parts were commingled with others' parts.

When addressing the *who*, there are three main scientific methods to positively identify remains:

- Fingerprints
- Teeth
- DNA

The term "positive identification" means the method used to identify the person is scientifically accepted as proof of that identification. Therefore, teeth identification is as accepted as fingerprints which are as accepted as DNA within the scientific community as an accurate and valid identification.

Other methods of identification are not considered absolute, so pathologists must rely on one of the above positive identification methods. Visual confirmation of remains is no longer counted as a positive ID. In stories, writers often have a friend or family member travel to the morgue to "identify the body." The problem is, be it from emotion, decomposition, or other reasons, too many misidentifications have occurred to rely on this method.

ACCURACY – Visual IDs are not reliable and are no longer considered a positive identification technique.

Similarly, the use of tattoos is also not considered a positive ID. Isn't it possible that another person selected that same tattoo (or one extremely comparable) from the artist's portfolio? That is why the three scientific methods listed above are the only confirmatory identification methods a pathologist uses. Let's go through each one:

Fingerprints
Fingerprinting a deceased person is much the same as fingerprinting a live person. At autopsy, an investigator inks the deceased's finger pads and rolls them onto a paper form to capture the unique patterns created by each pad's friction ridges.

FUN FACT – All persons, even identical twins, have unique fingerprints.

Different stages of decomposition can create obstacles in fingerprinting the deceased, however. **Skin slippage**, a decompositional effect discussed in Chapter 5, is the detachment of the outer layer of the skin from the body.

Sometimes skin slippage around the hands and feet can cause that entire section to detach at once, creating skin "gloves" and "socks" that fall from the body intact.

I told you I'd keep this book fun!

Because the inner layers of the skin do not have as pronounced ridge patterns as the surface skin, skin slippage makes fingerprinting a deceased person extremely difficult, if not impossible. However, investigators can use the loose skin layer itself to collect prints. They simply put each finger of the skin glove over their own fingers (wearing a latex glove) and roll it as if they are taking their own prints.

It normally doesn't matter if the investigator's hand is a different size than the deceased's hands. There is no problem if the skin glove tears, as long as the tears do not occur within the fingerprints. So if the investigator has to split the top or back of the fingers to make them fit on his hand, usable fingerprints can still be printed.

FUN FACT – If medical personnel can locate and save the skin glove, investigators can put it over their own hand (while wearing a latex glove, of course) and go through the motion of taking their own fingerprints, which actually creates perfect fingerprints for the deceased.

Other times the body becomes dried out, causing severe wrinkles in the finger pads, which obscure the friction ridges. This also makes obtaining usable prints almost impossible. In these cases the investigator can ask the pathologist to inject a **tissue builder** into the affected areas. A tissue builder is a solvent created to be thicker than water. The purpose of a tissue builder is to rehydrate and smooth out the shriveled, creased pads. If used correctly, a tissue builder will create pristine pads suitable for printing.

If the skin has not turned brittle, the investigator attending the autopsy can instead ask the pathologist to remove each of the wrinkled pads. As he receives each one, the investigator applies pressure to the back of the pad to smooth it out. As with skin slippage, he then puts the pad over his own finger (again, while wearing a glove) and takes the print that way. With this method, the investigator must take great care not to mix up the pads, so that each pad is printed in the appropriate space on the form.

Odontology

Teeth, when still a part of the skull, can also be used to positively identify remains. **Odontology** is the scientific study of teeth and their development and decay. I discuss odontology at length in Chapter 3 when I cover the different autopsy specialties.

A forensic odontologist can compare X-rays taken of the deceased with **antemortem** X-rays (X-rays from previous routine dentist visits) to make the ID. Tooth position and orientation, dental work, and filling shapes, are just a few of the comparisons he makes.

> TERMS – Antemortem is Latin for "before death." Antemortem medical records are medical data collected while the person was still alive.

Teeth that have been knocked out of the skull or have fallen out due to decomposition are not nearly as useful. That is not to say they have no value, but proving the teeth were from that skull or putting the teeth in the appropriate order/position becomes problematic when calling the identification a positive match.

DNA

DNA is the third scientifically accepted method for positively identifying remains. As with the other two methods, DNA is useful only if the analysts have something to compare it to. So there must be some sort of antemortem record from the deceased. Specifically for this purpose of identifying bodies, every person who serves in the US military provides a DNA sample. These samples are kept at the Armed Forces Institute of Pathology and are used by the Office of the Armed Forces Medical Examiner to identify military remains. Before I inadvertently inspire any inaccurate plot bunnies, however, I must stress that there are very strict rules regarding these samples.

Their only purpose and the only reason they can be used is to identify remains from military operations. These samples cannot be used by law enforcement in any criminal investigation, no matter how gruesome or sensationalized.

When taking DNA samples from a body, the pathologist typically collects specimens from the blood, bone, organs, muscle, and skin. She can also take oral swabs and pluck hair.

Final Medical Examinations

Probably the least recognized purpose of the forensic autopsy is to give the deceased his final thorough medical examination. This can be beneficial for a few reasons. First and foremost, a thorough examination can identify undiagnosed or misdiagnosed illness or disease that might be hereditary. Such genetic findings could be invaluable to close family members.

Another reason to do a complete exam is to secure against any future naysayers. A total examination eliminates any argument, no matter how farfetched, alleging the pathologist missed vital data that could have changed the cause of death.

In the Casey Anthony case I discussed previously, one of the criticisms Dr. Spitz had for Dr. G was that she did not open Caylee's head. Dr. G opined doing so would not have provided any useful information. Unfortunately, she only ended up opening herself to denigration.

Clinical Autopsy

The **clinical autopsy**, also referred to as the **hospital autopsy**, is far less thorough than a forensic autopsy. It is conducted to diagnose and chart the disease that led to death. These autopsies help create medical advances by expanding the understanding of a disease and determining why the medical efforts were ineffective.

In most clinical autopsies, the cause of death is known prior to the patient passing away, and therefore the death is neither unexplained nor suspicious as is required for a forensic autopsy. If the deceased was under a doctor's care prior to death, meaning he was being seen for the disease that killed him, the death is not considered unattended. Even if no one stood at his hospital bedside when the patient passed, the death is an attended one.

> TERMS – A clinical/hospital autopsy occurs for attended, expected deaths and strives to identify and track the fatal disease.

There are three primary reasons to conduct a hospital autopsy:

- To identify the disease that caused the death.
- To study the pathology of the disease.
- To provide a final, thorough medical examination for that person.

The clinical autopsy is typically conducted on-site at the medical facility where the patient died, or that was providing his primary care. The patient's primary physician is not normally the doctor conducting the autopsy, although all of his notes are reviewed and he is often personally consulted by the pathologist.

There are important differentiations between a clinical autopsy and a forensic postmortem:

- The next of kin <u>may request</u> a clinical autopsy, and likewise <u>may refuse or limit</u> the autopsy.
- The manner of death is not a consideration as all clinical autopsies should be natural deaths.
- The cause of death is often known while the patient is still alive.
- The coroner or medical examiner is not normally involved in the clinical autopsy process.
- The pathologist performing the clinical autopsy does not need to be forensically trained.

Should the next of kin request a clinical autopsy, they may be required to pay for it, which is an expensive venture as autopsies are typically not covered by medical insurance. Most hospitals, however, will do the clinical autopsy without charge if the person died within their facility.

If the hospital is providing the autopsy, they have on-staff pathologists assigned to the facility's morgue to conduct the procedure. If the family is paying for the autopsy, they can use the hospital's pathologist or hire their own. If they hire their own, the hospital is under no obligation to provide the use of their morgue.

As with the forensic autopsy, one of the primary objectives in performing a clinical autopsy is to provide a thorough, final medical examination for the person. However, the scope of the autopsy must have consent from the next of kin, who could limit it only to the area of the body most associated with the disease.

Since the clinical autopsy is often greatly focused, finding other causes of death are extremely rare. The pathologist is normally analyzing the disease that they already knew about. However, if a writer wanted to take a clinical autopsy and have the pathologist stumble across something unexpected, I'd allow those plot bunnies to run free! In those type of cases, the pathologist would typically reach out to the coroner/ME for assistance or advice.

Psychological Autopsy

In your research of autopsies, you may have come across the term "psychological autopsy," which is not a medical procedure at all. A **psychological autopsy** is conducted by a forensic psychologist and seeks to determine the mental state of the deceased in relation to the stressors in his life, to help identify a manner of death in undetermined cases. In the vast majority of psychological autopsies, suicides are confirmed.

> **TERMS** – The psychological autopsy is a mental health review of a deceased's life leading up to his death.

The psychological autopsy is an exhaustive investigation that includes thorough interviews of family, friends, and other people in the deceased's life, a review of his medical records to include any mental health records, and an evaluation of the events in his life that could have had any significant effect on him. The psychological autopsy attempts to reveal the deceased's state of mind during the weeks, days, and hours leading up to the death, and attempts to explain the actions the deceased took. Officially, the appropriate terminology for the psychological autopsy's objective is it attempts to describe the *proximate causation of the death.*

While at times an effective investigative tool, we must always evaluate this type of report with a degree of skepticism. While a medical autopsy takes into account the biological and tangible findings of the physical body, the psychological autopsy will always require the psychologist to enter the deceased's mind. Therefore, no matter how accurate, the findings will always be based in supposition. Further muddying the findings is the fact that there are no well-established standardizations or systematic guidelines concerning the methodology of psychological autopsies.

Some law enforcement agencies have a forensic psychologist on staff or retainer, however, most of the time investigators must seek out and hire a forensic psychologist if they desire a psychological autopsy for a particular case. Families can also hire forensic psychologists for this purpose. Pathologists deal with the physical autopsy and are not involved in the psychological autopsy process.

Second Autopsy

Sometimes, after the forensic autopsy is completed, an additional autopsy is conducted on the body using a different pathologist. Officially called a **second autopsy**, it can occur for a variety of reasons:

- The next of kin wish to pay for their own autopsy.
- A thorough autopsy was not conducted originally.
- New information was developed that was not on hand for the first autopsy.
- The lead investigating agency has further medical questions that were not addressed originally.
- Corruption has been alleged with either the coroner/medical examiner's office or the lead

investigating agency, and the investigation is starting anew.

Depending on the circumstances, the call for a second autopsy may occur immediately after the original autopsy or years after the fact. If the body has been buried, an exhumation must be approved by the presiding magistrate.

> **TERMS – Exhumation is the process of digging up a buried body.**

Every second autopsy inherently has its own limitations. The organs have often already been removed and dissected, so any analysis of how they were positioned at death is impossible. Also, the fluids required for toxicology evaluation are no longer available.

The second autopsy's pathologist must rely on the original pathologist's office to provide any tissue and fluid samples they kept from the first autopsy. While most coroners and medical examiners do keep such samples from each postmortem exam, the quality may be questionable, especially if the reason for the second autopsy is the alleged incompetence of the original office.

The benefit of the second autopsy is that it is always a completely thorough exam and often can discover vital evidence originally missed. For example, broken bones can lead investigators to investigate a homicide from an original SIDS case. Hair can still contain drug information. Antemortem injuries can still be distinguished from postmortem wounds. Depending on how well the original autopsy was conducted, the second autopsy can provide a plethora of information.

Reports

Each of the four types of autopsies described above provides an official document at the end called an **autopsy report**. In the physical autopsies, the autopsy report includes all of the physical injuries and identification marks found on the body. The mechanism of death is described in the body of the report. In forensic autopsies, the cause and manner of death are also annotated.

An autopsy report is not published until the entire autopsy is complete, which, as we'll discuss in Chapter 4, can take months when waiting on the lab reports. An autopsy is not considered finalized until the autopsy report is completed.

Autopsy reports are kept at the coroner or medical examiner's offices, filed with the case. Law enforcement and US attorneys/district attorneys routinely receive copies of these reports. As a governmental record, the public must go through a Freedom of Information Act process to gain access to the autopsy report.

> **TERMS** – The autopsy report lists all of the findings of the autopsy, including all injuries and the cause and manner of death. It includes toxicological and histological findings and therefore cannot be signed until those laboratory functions are complete, which could take months.

A **death certificate** is provided by a medical doctor for all deaths. In forensic autopsies, it is signed by the coroner or medical examiner. For attended deaths, it is issued by the attending doctor. The death certificate lists all of the patient's personal history information, including age, sex, race, family history, and disposition of the body (burial or cremation). The cause of death is also annotated, usually as a primary cause and then includes any secondary factors. In forensic autopsies, the coroner or medical examiner marks the manner of death. There is also a section for the doctor to annotate the time of death. The death certificate is essential for the mortician to take possession of the body and also for insurance companies to process life insurance claims.

> **TERMS** – A death certificate is a validation that the person listed died, and must therefore be filled out by a doctor.

An important distinction should be made when talking about a doctor validating that a body is indeed dead. This is called the **declaration of death**, which is the time the declaration is noted. This is separate and distinct, however, from the **time-of-death estimate**, which is the window of time within which the pathologist concludes the person actually died. Time-of-death estimates are covered in Chapter 6.

So if a person died on the operating table, the time of the declaration of death and the time of death are the same. However, when a body is discovered at a death scene, the declaration of death is the current time, while the time-of-death window will be sometime earlier.

PITFALL – Do not confuse a declaration of death and a time of death in your writing. There are instances when they share the same time, but they are still distinct statistics and do not mean the same thing.

The death certificate is filed with the county clerk and becomes a county record. Each state has varying rules on when such records become public records.

Depending on the final disposition of the body, the funeral director obtains a **burial permit**. This is a legal document that must be applied for, which authorizes burial, cremation, or the scattering of ashes. In most counties, the burial permit becomes part of the death certificate and is filed with the county's records. Other states file the two documents separately, but both are still with the county clerk.

Case Study 1: Ryan Jenkins – Implanted Evidence

Ryan Alexander Jenkins was a thirty-two-year-old unemployed man from a wealthy family, originally from Calgary, Canada. 2009 found Ryan in Las Vegas, NV, searching for fame and fortune while living off of money from his father, Dan Jenkins.

Ryan frequented casino parties and presented himself as a successful, self-made millionaire, which caught the attention of producers casting for a reality show. In February 2009, Ryan participated as a contestant on the VH-1 show, *Megan Wants a Millionaire*, a *Bachlorette*-inspired series in Los Angeles. Ryan came in third.

According to interviews, Ryan was disappointed he didn't win the cash prize. He went back to Las Vegas, desperate to make money and joined the poker circuit. A few weeks later, on March 16, 2009, in one of the casinos, he met Jasmine Fiore, a twenty-eight-year-old card dealer and failed actress. Jasmine, too, was looking to make her fortune, and was frustrated at her lack of success. She settled for dating rich men around the Las Vegas area.

Two days later, Ryan and Jasmine married at the Little White Wedding Chapel on the Las Vegas Strip. Allegedly, Ryan married Jasmine for the money she had saved, while friends reported Jasmine married Ryan because he claimed he was facing visa issues and wanted to stay in the United States. He also promised Jasmine his "fortune."

Ryan wanted to be visible in the Las Vegas scene, so he attended several parties with Jasmine, who, from friends' accounts, was getting suspicious of Ryan. He frequently asked Jasmine to pay the bills for their extravagant living, while telling her it took time to release his fortune into US currency.

In June 2009, Ryan and Jasmine were at another party where Jasmine openly flirted with another man. Ryan hit Jasmine in her arm and threw her into the pool. Jasmine filed a police report and Ryan spent two days in jail. Shortly after, Jasmine moved to Los Angeles to get away from Ryan, but he quickly followed her and she let him move back in.

While in Los Angeles, Ryan was cast for another reality show, the third season of *I Love Money*, and in July 2009, went to Mexico to begin shooting. While he was away, Jasmine began researching annulling their marriage, and reconnected with an old wealthy boyfriend, Robert Hasman. When Ryan returned after the show wrapped, he wooed Jasmine back by telling her he had won the competition and the $250,000 grand prize.

On Thursday, August 13, 2009, Ryan and Jasmine drove down to Del Mar, CA, just north of San Diego, for a poker tournament held at the Del Mar Hilton. They checked into the L'Auberge Hotel in Del Mar.

After a night of poker and discos, Ryan checked out of the hotel, alone, the next morning, Friday, at 9:20 AM. The following day, Saturday, Ryan texted several of Jasmine's friends asking if they'd seen her. That night, although he claimed he received a text from Jasmine stating she was in Santa Barbara, CA, Ryan called the Los Angeles Police Department and reported her missing.

Unbeknownst to Ryan, although not yet identified, Jasmine's body had been discovered almost fourteen hours earlier in Buena Park, CA, a suburb of Los Angeles that is on the way to San Diego. A resident found the body in a suitcase dripping blood in his apartment building's dumpster. The body was missing all of its teeth and fingers.

The Orange County Coroner performed a thorough forensic autopsy on the remains and found the body had been badly beaten in the head and then strangled, which was the cause of death. He faced a dilemma with identifying the body, however, and concluded the teeth and fingers had been intentionally removed to hide the body's identity. He had an innovative idea, though, when he remembered that breast implants contain unique serial numbers. The coroner removed Jasmine's implants and was able to identify her by those serial numbers on Tuesday, August 18.

This quick identification proved to be invaluable in this case because later that same day, when the Buena Park Police Department attempted to find Ryan for questioning, he was already on the run. Had the identification been slowed by even a day, Ryan could have made it to one of several properties his family owned in nonextradition countries.

The LAPD reported to the Buena Park police that earlier that day, they, too, had reached out to Ryan to ask follow-up questions on the missing person case he filed, not knowing his wife had been identified by the coroner. Ryan called them back and said he was out of town and heading to Canada because he had issues with his visa. Witnesses later reported he hooked his boat to the back of his SUV for the trip.

From video footage and other evidence, Buena Park detectives were able to piece together the events from Ryan's August 13 Del Mar trip:

- Video footage shows Ryan and Jasmine checking into the L'Auberge Hotel at 3:30 PM. The suitcase they had was the same luggage Jasmine was found in.
- Security footage from the hallway of their

room shows them leaving at 6:30 PM, dressed up for the poker tournament.

- Text messages show Jasmine was texting Robert Hasman, making plans to leave Ryan while Ryan was playing poker that night.
- Jasmine's car, which they drove to Del Mar, was found about a mile away from Jasmine's condo in Los Angeles. A significant amount of Jasmine's blood and hair was found inside. This suggests that after the night clubs, but before getting back to the hotel that night, Ryan beat Jasmine in the car.
- Jasmine's blood and hair were also discovered on the back patio of Ryan's L'Auberge Hotel room. Detectives assume Ryan did not want to take a beaten Jasmine through the hotel lobby, so tried to take her through his room's back door, but it was locked. So he left her on the patio until he could unlock it.
- Security video shows Ryan running to his room at 4:30 AM, Friday morning, alone. At this point he most likely unlocked the back door and retrieved Jasmine.
- At 5:00 AM the hallway camera records Ryan exiting the room with the phone handset and the ice bucket. He hides the handset in the hallway and then retrieves ice before going back into his room. This suggests he did not

want anyone using the room's phone, implying Jasmine was still alive at this time.

- At 6:30 AM the hallway footage shows Ryan leaving the room, alone, carrying clothes and what appears to be a toiletry kit. Taking the contents of the suitcase out of the room without the suitcase implies he needed it empty. This probably means Jasmine was dead at this point, strangled between 5:00 and 6:30 AM.
- At 9:20 AM Ryan leaves the room for the last time, alone, with no luggage, and checks out of the hotel. This implies he took the suitcase to the car via the room's back door. He most likely used the suitcase to store Jasmine's body so he would not be seen carrying her.
- Jasmine's body was discovered in Buena Park, which is on the way from Del Mar to Los Angeles. Somewhere, either at the hotel or during the trip before he dumped her body, Ryan pulled out her teeth and cut off her fingers.
- The security cameras at Jasmine's condo, where Ryan was living, show Ryan arriving at the complex on foot. As mentioned above, Jasmine's car was later discovered in a parking lot about a mile away.
- The next day, Saturday, Ryan texts Jasmine's

friends asking about her whereabouts and also texts himself from Jasmine's phone, saying she's in Santa Barbara. Records show both Ryan's and Jasmine's phones were pinging off the same cell tower in Los Angeles, not Santa Barbara, at the time of the texts.

- Saturday night, Ryan reports Jasmine as a missing person.

The Buena Park Police Department issued a warrant for Ryan's arrest and put out an all-points bulletin in an attempt to stop him from crossing the border into Canada. Canadian police detained Ryan's father, Dan, and made it obvious any aid he provided would lead to Ryan's capture.

Police eventually found Ryan's SUV and empty boat trailer near Blaine, Washington. Detectives believe he crossed into Canada using his boat in the night hours of August 19 – 20. On the evening of August 20, with the help of an unidentified female, Ryan checked into the Thunderbird Motel in Hope, British Columbia, Canada. On August 23, after Ryan failed to check out, the manager entered the room and found Ryan hanging by his belt off the clothes rack, dead.

Had it not been for the quick thinking and identification of Jasmine's remains by the coroner during her autopsy, Ryan would have had plenty of time to get to his father in Canada and then escape to a nonextradition country. Without Jasmine's identity, detectives would not have been able to connect Ryan to the crime, and would not have had any reason to trace his movements during the Del Mar trip. The autopsy was key in cracking this case.

Out of respect to the Fiore family, *Megan Wants a Millionaire* was canceled after only three episodes, and Ryan's season of *I Love Money* never aired at all.

Chapter 3: The Autopsy –
External Examination

Serials from *Quincy, M.E.* to *Bones,* and from *Six Feet Under* to *iZombie* place their weekly tales of angst and intrigue in morgues and mortuaries. But what happens there? How does a writer move a body from on-page extra to vital story participant? In this chapter, we'll begin following the body in the step-by-step procedure of an autopsy.

The forensic autopsy process begins once the body arrives at the morgue. The information needed to produce a thorough, conclusive autopsy report requires considerable examination of the body before any cutting actually occurs. For this reason, I have divided the autopsy procedure into two chapters, split between the external and internal body examinations.

Because the full forensic autopsy goes beyond the scalpel, there are several other practices that are involved, with their own team of specialists. These forensic specialties include:

- Photography
- Radiology
- Odontology
- Anthropology
- Entomology
- Pathology
- Toxicology
- Histology

Some offices, especially medical examiner offices, have these specialists on-staff and available. Some do not and must hire these specialists on a case-by-case basis. If you're looking for real life accuracy in your story, do research into the local office covering the area you are writing about. If you want to take creative liberty regarding who is on-staff and what specialists are available when creating your own fictional morgue, you should be able to do so without criticism, keeping in mind that all offices have at least pathologists, radiologists, and photographers.

I will discuss each of the forensic specialties as I go through the autopsy process. The final three in the list, forensic pathology, toxicology, and histology, will be covered in the next chapter, where I'll discuss the internal body examination.

Vocabulary

Vocabulary? Again? Haven't you had enough words? *Nah.* Writers can never have too many words. The pathologists and other specialists involved in autopsies use medical lingo heavily in their conversations, diagnoses, and reports. For a writer, though, vocabulary can be a tricky thing. Correct terminology can bring authenticity to the story, but on the other hand, risks losing the reader if it's incomprehensible.

I want to give you as much vocabulary as possible to help bring credibility to your writing. I encourage you, however, to be mindful of your usage. An on-point Latin phrase loses its luster if it only serves to frustrate the reader. So, with yellow caution lights blinking, here we go.

When describing a body, it is important to realize that the orientation is <u>always</u> from the body's point of view. When looking at the body's face, his right eye is to your left. Likewise, when face up, his left kidney is to your right. When the body is turned over, however, the body's left and right correspond with yours. Care must be taken, then, when describing injuries. They, too, are <u>always</u> described from the body's POV.

The body's front is referred to as the **anterior**, while its back is the **posterior**. The line down the center of the body is called the **medial**, while the side of the body is called the **lateral**.

When evaluating injuries or artifacts (such as scars or tattoos), the pathologist must describe their location in proximity to known body parts. Towards the head is **superior**, while towards the feet is

inferior. Likewise, on the limbs, towards the torso (the beginning of the arm or leg) is **proximal**, and towards the end of the limb (the hand or foot) is **distal**.

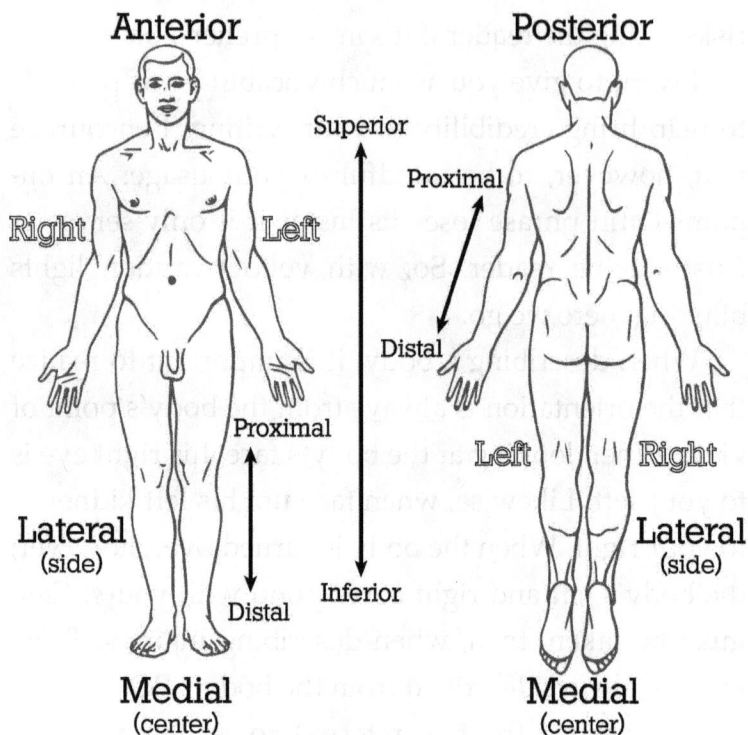

Figure 1: Medical Terms

I will cover phrases used to describe the organs in the next chapter when we discuss the internal examination portion of the autopsy.

When using these terms, they are descriptors much like east and west are contextual descriptors. When asked for one's location, the answer isn't simply "east." The answer is "I'm three miles east of the hotel." The same logic is applied to these medical terms to situate the information provided. An injury isn't "superior," it is "two inches superior to the navel." A scar may be two centimeters proximal to the left inner elbow. And so on.

Personal Protective Equipment

Although I may not mention personal protective equipment (PPE) as I go through each step of the autopsy procedure, realize that it is an important guard against bloodborne pathogens, disease, and other contagions, and is worn at all times.

PPE is any of a variety of disposable outer clothing. Depending on the situation, the professionals using PPE can choose from latex gloves, shoe booties, sleeves, aprons, goggles, masks, and full out biohazard "bunny suits" (*yes, really*).

Some morgues and mortuaries have specific requirements of what will be worn when. Some leave it to the doctors and technicians themselves to decide how much PPE to wear given the risks of that stage of the autopsy. In my experience, gloves, sleeves, aprons and booties were required wear, with masks and goggles used when cutting bone. Rarely are full bunny suits required.

The Autopsy

As I now take you through each of the stages of the

autopsy, please keep in mind that it can be run slightly differently office to office, depending on the attending coroner or medical examiner.

> **ACCURACY –** Most autopsies are conducted in the order laid out in this book, but keep in mind small variances may exist office to office.

The process I lay out below is from my experiences with the Baltimore Medical Examiner's Office, the Cook County Medical Examiner's Office, and the Office of the Armed Forces Medical Examiner, as well as my research into other offices. Using the flow described below for the process will bring validity to your book, but if you want absolute accuracy, you need to do specific research into the specific office and region you're writing about. If you want to make changes in the order of some of the steps for your story's purposes, no one should challenge you on that.

Intake

As touched on in Chapter 1, this entire process begins when the coroner or medical examiner receives notification of a suspicious death. Bodies at death scenes are off-limits to law enforcement personnel. They must wait until the coroner or medical examiner's representative arrives on the scene. This representative can be the coroner or medical examiner herself, an on-staff deputy coroner or medical examiner, or an appointed on-duty local medical representative, depending on how that office has its process set up. There may also be a photographer assigned to respond as well, but not always, as the pathologist can get copies of the crime scene investigators' photos.

At the scene, the representative evaluates the body, declares death and annotates the time, puts the remains into a body bag, and transports them to the morgue.

Most coroners and medical examiners do not conduct the autopsy immediately upon the body's arrival. Were that the case, their days would be too choppy and they would never be able to schedule any of their other duties. Instead, most offices put each body collected during that day and night into the cooler, a refrigerated room, where the body is kept overnight. In the morning, the coroner or medical examiner autopsies each of the stored bodies and then spends the rest of her day filling out reports or accomplishing her other tasks.

> FUN FACT – Most bodies are kept in a refrigerated room at around 38 degrees Fahrenheit so that decomposition is significantly slowed and the body can be held until the next day for autopsy, without the risk of freezing it.

Each office is set up according to the coroner or

chief medical examiner. So, as stated before, it's possible for some offices to follow different procedures. Likewise, it's possible for the coroner/ME to decide not to wait until the next day for specific corpses. Due to political pressure or the high-visibility of certain cases, the coroner/ME may decide to conduct the autopsy immediately. All of the following steps are still followed, the remains just aren't stored overnight with the rest of the bodies. In most offices, these exceptions are rare, as they disrupt the day's schedule, but writers should feel free to disrupt as needed.

Upon its arrival at the morgue, technicians catalog the body according to the office's numbering system and create a folder that holds any documentation that came with the remains. This includes medical records, preliminary law enforcement reports, or anything else that could be significant for the pathologist.

Make note that the cataloging number the morgue generates is different than the investigation case number law enforcement uses. If one incident resulted in three bodies, for example, they would all be part of the same law enforcement investigation. However, at the morgue, three separate catalogue numbers would be generated, one for each body. The pathologist treats each body as its own case.

Before being replaced by modern techniques, toe tags used to serve as the primary cataloging method.

The unique morgue number for the body as well as other physical stats, such as gender, height, and weight, were recorded on a cardboard label and then attached via string onto the body's big toe. This way the body was marked and identified with the catalog information without it being in the way of the autopsy procedure.

Toe tags are no longer used. In my experience, the gurney that the body is on is marked with all of the catalog information. In some morgues a wristband with a barcode is generated and put on the body's wrist.

ACCURACY – Although many writers still use toe tags in their books for effect (like on the cover of this one!), they are really a relic of an earlier time. Bodies are still cataloged and tracked, but not by tying a cardboard tag on the toe.

The techs then unzip the body bag and open it so the entire body is exposed. The morgue photographer takes overall pictures of the clothed body and close-up shots of anything of interest.

These photos are important as proof of how the body looked and its condition when it came into the care of the coroner or medical examiner. While the body bag's zipper is opened and out of the way, the radiologist also takes X-rays. The body is then stored overnight in the cooler.

In mass casualty situations, intake is treated as a triage. The bodies are all still cataloged, photographed, X-rayed, and stored, but flow control becomes exceedingly important. All gurneys must be adequately labeled with the correct catalog number, and all records, including the intake folder and the X-rays, must remain on the appropriate gurney. Carelessness could result in the wrong records going with the wrong remains, and could create significant confusion.

In mass casualties where commingling of remains occurred as a result of the fatal incident, initial photos of the remains in the body bag are extremely important to show how the mixture of remains arrived and what other remains they were found with.

Radiology

Radiology is the official name for the specialty of taking X-rays, also called **radiographs**. To be completely correct, it deals with all sorts of radiation imagery, including gamma rays, but for this topic, X-rays are the focus.

> **FUN FACT –** The "X" in X-ray comes from the algebraic concept of "X," which represents an unknown. It was labeled as such because when X-ray radiation was first discovered, they didn't know exactly what it was. Yay, math!

Overlapping X-rays so that they cover the entire body is an important step in the autopsy process. The images give the attending pathologist an internal view of the body before she has to cut. They allow her to document broken bones and internal injuries and focus her examination. In shooting victims, X-rays also reveal what bullets are in the body and where. This way, the pathologist knows where to recover the bullets and also is protected against missing any.

As mentioned above, the X-rays are collected at intake, after the photographer is done. It is important for the body bag to remain unzipped so the metal zipper is out of the way and won't cover any part of the body in the radiograph. The X-rays, while really used just prior to the internal examination, are taken the previous day because there is significant time involved in taking the X-rays and then developing the radiographs. This way, all of that is done at intake and ready for the doctor when she begins her assessment of the body.

At the Office of the Armed Forces Medical Examiner, X-rays are also taken prior to the morgue technicians unzipping the body bags. That office receives many American military remains from overseas locations. This step allows the office to detect any potential booby traps on the body.

Odontology

I wrote about odontology, which is forensic dentistry,

in the last chapter when I listed the methods of positively identifying remains. Because odontology is the analysis of the teeth and their positioning in the skull, when applied to the identification of remains, forensic dentists have two requirements. First, and obviously, there must be teeth in the skull. If the face of the deceased has been crushed or is not with the body, or if the deceased has no teeth, identification by odontology cannot occur. Second, the odontologist needs antemortem dental records of the person to compare the teeth to.

The odontolgist does his analysis by taking dental X-rays, making casts of the teeth, and in some rare but extreme situations, by removing the lower jaw. It should be noted, though, that the jaw can only be removed once the option for an open-casket funeral has already been denied by the pathologist due to the severity and type of injuries, normally to the face. The odontologist's work cannot be the reason that an open casket is not possible.

Another area where forensic odontology is invaluable is in cases involving bite marks. If a body has bite mark injuries, the odontologist can analyze and document the shapes and positioning of the marks. Once a suspect is identified, the odontologist can make a casting of his teeth and then compare the cast to the injury to determine if they match. Naturally, this process can be done on bite victims who are still alive as well.

Anthropology

Bodies are not always delivered to the morgue in pristine condition. Depending on how long the person has been dead, as well as the environmental conditions the remains were exposed to, the body might be severely decomposed or even reduced to skeletal remains. For these situations, a forensic anthropologist may be used to analyze the remains.

Forensic anthropology is the study of bones in order to discern the likely demographic stats for that person. An anthropologist can determine a person's probable gender, age range, race, stature, developmental handicaps, and skeletal injuries that can all help identify the body.

Various bone features go into determining the gender of a skeletonized body. Because female bodies support pregnancy, their pelvic bones have a wider opening with a more circular shape than the male pelvis. The **sacrum**, which connects the pelvis to the tailbone (called the **coccyx**), also differs between genders, as females have a distinctly shorter sacrum. Anthropologists can also determine gender from the skull. In males, the skull is typically larger and has a more prominent forehead.

For age determinations, anthropologists have an easier time estimating childhood ranges. In humans, various bones continue to grow, fuse, and develop until the age of twenty-five, and these can be plotted out on growth charts. After that, the bones have finished developing and age determinations are much more difficult.

The anthropologist has to rely on either osteons or arthritis development for their adult estimations. **Osteons** are microscopic growths within the bone's structure. Although the bones stop growing at maturity, they continue to produce osteons over a person's lifetime. Therefore, young adults tend to have fewer but larger osteons, while older adults have many more osteons that are smaller.

A body's genetic heritage is typically determined through the characteristics of the skull. The eye sockets and nasal cavities tend to be distinct depending on genealogy.

The genetics of mixed races can get complicated. Normally, each feature will be provided by one of the parents. Rarely, there can be a mixture of a feature. Dominant and recessive gene pools and the mixtures of genetics goes beyond the scope of this text. I just want you to understand that forensic anthropologists use all of their findings to build a profile of the person's features, which aid in identifying the person.

Forensic anthropologists can also perform **facial reconstructions** to approximate what the deceased look like. Facial reconstruction uses the body's skull and estimates the various tissue widths based on the perceived age, race, and gender. Clay is then added to the skull in these widths to create a face.

Entomology

Entomology is the study of insects, whose presence can greatly assist in the external examination of a body. The body provides a moist, protected area to colonize, while also acting as a never-ending food source. Therefore, insects will use any accessible orifice (nostrils, ear canals, mouth, eyes, anus, and genitals, if exposed) to gain access into the body. They will also use open wounds. Since advanced decomposition processes (discussed in Chapter 5) can make wounds difficult to find, insect colonization away from any of the natural orifices helps identify injuries on the body.

Insects can also be used in toxicological analysis, which is the specialty that identifies drugs and toxins in the body. When insects feed off of flesh, they also ingest any drugs present there. Toxicologists can grind up these bugs and search for those drugs. A trained forensic entomologist should photograph, collect, and thoroughly label the insects present.

Probably the most significant contribution entomologists make to death investigations are time-of-death estimations. This process is explained fully in Chapter 6.

External Examination

Once all of the other specialists finish their processes with the body, it is then ready for the forensic pathologist. Her first step is to remove the body from the body bag and strip it of all its clothing. At this point, law enforcement can collect anything with evidentiary value. Everything else, called **personal effects**, including jewelry, clothing, wallets, purses, and whatever else was on the body at intake, is set aside for the next of kin.

> **TERMS** – "Personal effects" refers to the property (including clothing) brought in with the body, which, unless taken as evidence or verified as belonging to someone else, is released to the next of kin.

Before ever reaching for the scalpel, the pathologist must first conduct a thorough scalp-to-toe examination. She is looking for any artifact, which could be an injury, identifying birthmark, tattoo, or any item she deems of interest. She looks in the deceased's hair, under the eyelids, in the mouth, and examines every inch of skin. If she finds something unusual, she marks it on the **autopsy chart**, which is a male, female, or child figure (whichever is appropriate) on a piece of paper. She then turns the body over and does the same scalp-to-toe search on the posterior side.

Keep in mind that every corpse gets a unique catalogue number upon intake to the morgue. Since each morgue number is only one body, only one autopsy chart goes with each morgue case.

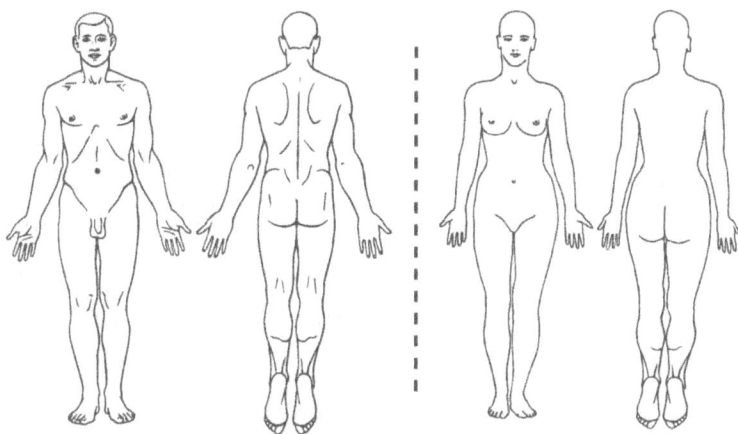

Figure 2: Male and Female Autopsy Charts

During this external examination, the pathologist typically allows law enforcement to collect evidence (other than the physical property which they collected already) from the body itself. The attending investigator often takes fingerprints of the deceased. However, this process can also be done by the coroner's/ME's own investigator if that office has one. The attending investigator may also ask the pathologist to collect fingernail scrapings or clippings, or to remove debris from the hair. The investigator takes all of these as evidence with him when he leaves.

If the coroner or medical examiner has an on-staff investigator, or if there is an autopsy where no physical evidence is expected, the law enforcement investigators may opt not to attend at all. It's really up to the investigator whether he feels he should attend, but if there is evidence, it's in his best interest to be present to collect it. Otherwise, he's leaving it to the coroner's/ME's office to do the collecting, which could potentially come under scrutiny by the defense at trial.

While some investigators stay for the entire two- to four-hour autopsy process, most leave after the evidence has been collected. What they need from the pathologist is the final autopsy report, and that cannot be completed until after all of the laboratory analysis is done, which may occur months later.

After the thorough external body inspection, the pathologist is now ready to cut into the remains. This begins the internal examination, which I cover in the next chapter.

Chapter 4: The Autopsy – Internal Examination

After the external analysis has been thoroughly documented, the pathologist turns her attention to the internal examination, which is the forensic pathology portion of the autopsy, and assuming there are no complexities, should take between two to four hours to complete. She first thoroughly inspects the X-rays for anything of note. Then she turns the body face-up and places a rubber block, approximately the size of a half loaf of bread, under the middle of the back, just beneath the shoulder blades. This body block extends and exaggerates the body's natural arch and provides easier access to both the chest and abdomen. She then begins the dissection process.

As in the previous chapters, as I go through this stage of the autopsy, I will be defining medical terms commonly used for each step.

Gaining Access

The first step is to gain access to the **thoracic cavity** (also called the chest cavity) and the abdomen. A **cavity** is an empty, hollow space. That's why a tooth cavity is filled with the mixture of metals called, obviously, a filling. It fills a hole (cavity) in your tooth.

> PITFALL – A common misconception is the human body is 98% water, leading some laypersons to believe we are walking water balloons with submerged organs that will spew our contents forth in a violent spray if punctured. The adult body is actually only about 60% water, and that's found in the body's tissues. The organs themselves mostly hang in empty spaces, cavities, within our bodies.

The **thorax** (chest) and abdomen contain most of the internal organs, including:

- Thoracic Cavity
  - Heart
  - Lungs
- Abdominal Cavity
  - Liver
  - Kidneys
  - Gallbladder
  - Stomach
  - Spleen
  - Small Intestine
  - Large Intestine

The pathologist reaches these organs by cutting through the skin and muscle. The pattern she uses for the cut is called a **Y-incision**, named so because the final cut looks like the letter Y. She makes the first cut from the shoulder to the bottom of the **sternum** (middle of the chest). She then makes a second cut from the other shoulder to the sternum, meeting the first cut. For female bodies, each of these cuts need to go around and under the breasts.

> **TERMS –** The sternum is also referred to as the breast-bone. It is the flat bone that runs down the center of the chest and connects all of the ribs.

From the meeting point at the sternum, the pathologist then cuts straight down the center of the body to the groin.

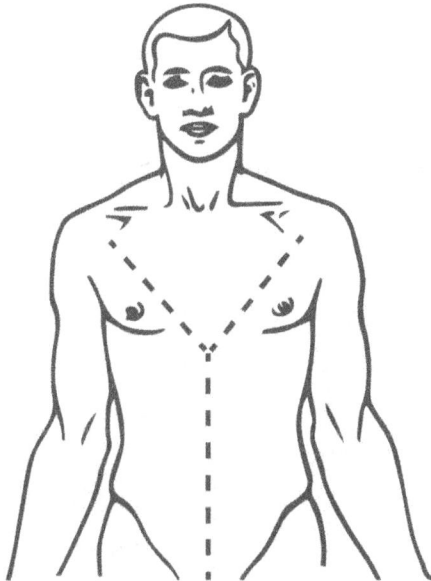

Figure 3: Y-incision

The specialized blade used to make the cuts is called a **scalpel**, and is the typical knife used in medical procedures. The skin and muscle of the human body are quite resilient and cannot be cut through to the bone in one motion. But the pathologist continues cutting the pattern until the Y-incision is all the way through.

Figure 4: Scalpel

The reason the incision is not simply a straight cut from throat to groin is that the pathologist must have full access to the rib cage, which protects the upper organs and acts as a barrier to the doctor. She must fully expose the rib cage so that she can remove it. To do this, she cuts back each of the three flesh flaps (top, right, and left) created by the Y-incision.

Once the ribs are exposed, the pathologist examines them before removing them. She looks for any breaks or abnormalities via X-rays, touch, and direct examination. Everything she finds could have significance in putting the story together. For example, a nick in a rib could indicate where the bullet hit the person in a shooting case, and could explain why it changed direction within the body. In infants, several ribs broken at the lateral portions (sides) of the body could indicate the child was a victim of shaken baby syndrome.

The ribs are made of both bone and cartilage, and therefore are not easy to cut through. The scalpel does not do the job. To remove the breastbone, some coroners and medical examiners use what is called a bone saw or **rib saw**. Using this saw, they cut along the cartilage/bone boundary at the front of the ribs (see Figure 7), which frees the breastbone for removal.

Figure 5: Rib Saw

Alternatively, and the practice I experienced in all of the autopsies I've personally been involved with, the pathologist can use pruning shears, in this case called **rib cutters**. This tool makes cutting through the bone much easier and allows the pathologist to snip each rib at the sides of the chest cavity (also shown in Figure 7).

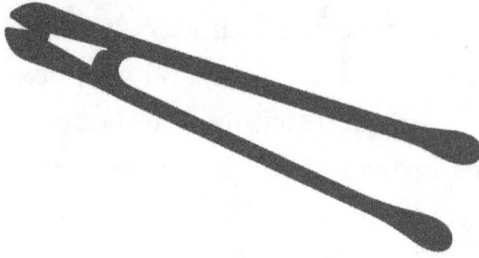

Figure 6: Rib Cutters

This way, the anterior portions of the ribs are removed with the breastbone, and the pathologist has far greater access to the thoracic cavity. Also, because the cuts are focused solely on the ribs themselves, there is no danger of sawing too hard and accidentally damaging the organs below, which needs to be considered when using a rib saw.

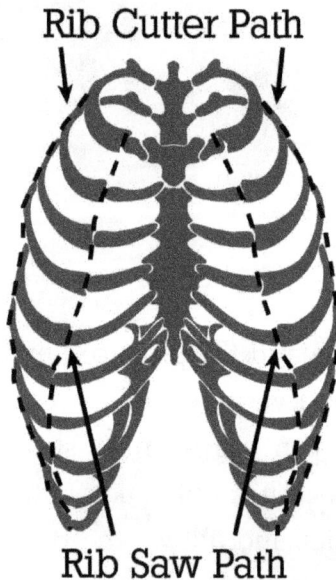

Rib Cutter Path

Rib Saw Path

Figure 7: Ribs and Cuts

Organs

Once the breastbone is removed, all of the body's organs, minus the brain, are accessible. The pathologist begins a systematic evaluation of each organ, removing it, weighing it, and inspecting it for abnormalities. She will slice into each organ to view the under-tissue, again searching for anything out of the ordinary. She will also take and preserve several samples of each organ, stored separately.

Samples of organs are taken for the following reasons:

- Toxicology screenings (drugs and poisons tests)
- Histology analysis (microscopic evaluations)
- Preservation (reexamination purposes – such as for second autopsies)

Body fluids, such as blood, bile, urine, and the vitreous humor (the eyeball fluid), are also preserved for toxicology and reexamination purposes. The pathologist also empties the contents of the stomach and intestines for examination. Please keep in mind that for a forensic autopsy to be considered completely thorough, especially in cases that require a diagnosis of exclusion, the pathologist must also examine the body's major glands and vessels during the internal examination process.

To make this process accessible, I'm going to walk

you through each of the organs and give basic information on each, such as typical size and weight. I'm also going to cover the basics of the medical jargon used for each. For example, no autopsy report will read the "heart stopped." Instead, the correct verbiage is "cardiac arrest." Unless your story will address a specific organ, or you are simply curious about anatomy, you may skip the rest of this section.

> **ALERT** – The following section becomes more technical than most writers need for their stories. It covers different specifics for each organ. Those writers who only need to know the autopsy procedure can skip ahead to the next section titled "Head Dissection."

Heart

- Approximately 10 ounces/280 grams (full grown).
- Approximately the size of a fist.
- Dense muscle tissue.
- Located in the thoracic cavity (chest), surrounded by the lungs.
- Creates blood pressure to move the blood throughout the body.
- Medical terminology starts with "cardi-". Examples:
  - Cardiology – the study of the heart
  - Cardiovascular system – the physiology of

the heart, arteries, veins, and capillaries, providing blood to the entire body.
- ○ Cardiac arrest – the heart stopped.

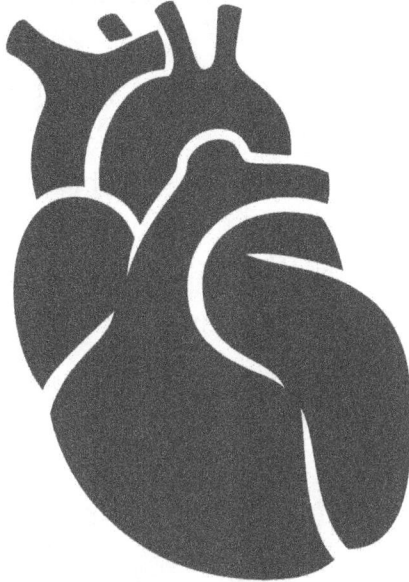

Figure 8: Heart

Lungs

- Right lung is bigger than the left lung.
  - ○ Right lung has three lobes.
  - ○ Left lung has two lobes, to make room for the heart.
- Together, approximately 3 pounds/1.5 kilograms (full grown).
  - ○ Right lung is a bit heavier than the left.
- Approximately as tall as a 20-ounce soft drink bottle.

- Spongy feel.
- Located in the thoracic cavity.
- Takes in air to oxygenate the blood.
- Medical terminology starts with "pulmo-". Examples:
  - Pulmonary medicine – care directed to fight lung disease.
  - Pulmonary arteries – the blood vessels carrying blood to the lungs for oxygenation.
  - Pulmonary embolism – blood pathway blockage in the lungs.

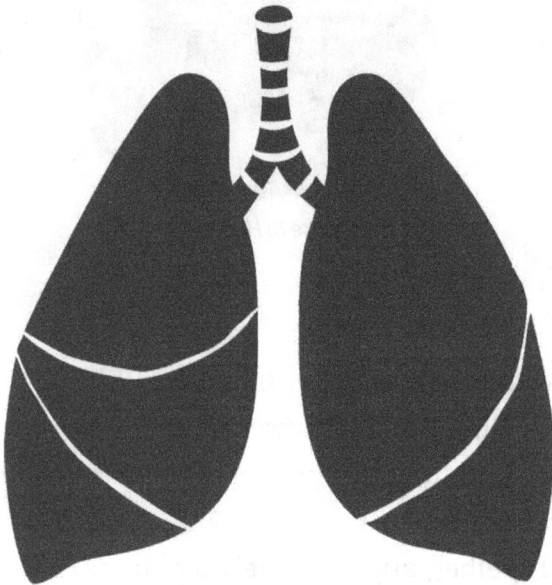

Figure 9: Lungs

Liver

- Largest internal organ.
- Approximately 3 pounds/1.5 kilograms (full grown).
- Approximately the size of a flattened football.
- Located in the upper right area of the abdominal cavity, directly beneath the diaphragm, which separates the abdomen from the thoracic cavity.
- Breaks down fat cells to create energy, breaks down old blood cells, and creates proteins.
- The only human organ that can regenerate.
- Medical terminology starts with "hepa-". Examples:
  - Hepatitis – the inflammation (swelling) of the liver.
  - Hepatoma – a tumor in the liver.

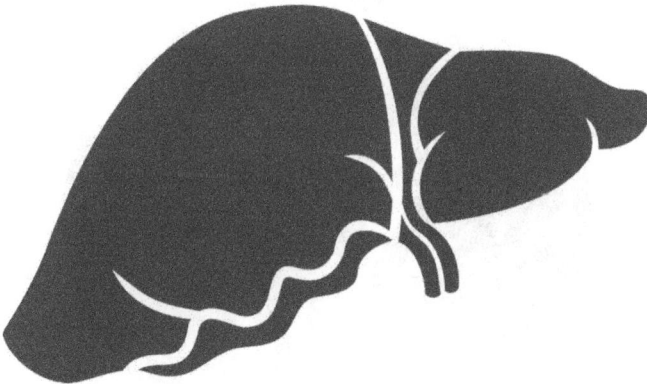

Figure 10: Liver

Kidneys

- Approximately 5 ounces/142 grams (each).
- Each, approximately the size of a deck of cards.
- Located below the liver and in the back of the abdominal cavity.
- Filters waste from the blood several times a day, and creates urine.
- Humans can survive with one kidney.
- Medical terminology starts with "nephro-" or "rena-". Examples:
  - Nephrologist – a doctor who studies the wellness of the kidneys.
  - Nephrosis – many types of kidney disease.
  - Chronic renal failure – the kidneys are not functioning properly.
  - Renal clearance tests – medical tests to see what wastes the kidneys are filtering.

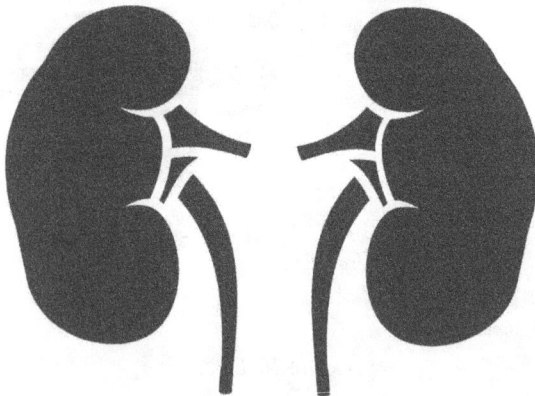

Figure 11: Kidneys

Gallbladder

- Approximately 2.5 ounces/71 grams.
- Looks like a small pear, approximately three inches long.
- Located directly below the liver.
- Stores bile, which it secretes into the small intestine to help digest fats.
- Humans can survive without the gallbladder.
- Medical terminology starts with "chole-". Examples:
  - Cholecystitis – inflammation of the gallbladder, often due to infection.
  - Cholescintigraphy – an examination of the gallbladder for live patients that uses a radioactive dye injected into the bile.

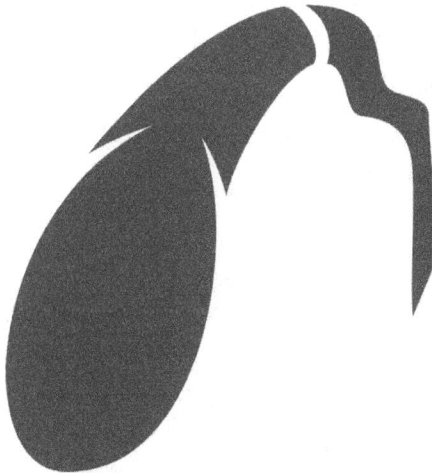

Figure 12: Gallbladder

Stomach

- Approximately 1.5 pounds/690 grams.
- The size of the stomach varies greatly person to person.
- Overeating can create larger stomachs.
- Can hold up to a gallon/4 liters of liquid.
- Located in the upper left of the abdominal cavity.
- Receives food from the esophagus, contains acids to start digestion, and releases food to the small intestine.
- Medical terminology starts with "gastr-". Examples:
  - Gastrointestinal – pertaining to the stomach and intestines.
  - Gastroesophageal reflux – Acid reflux, stomach contents that travel back up the esophagus.
  - Gastric ulcer – erosion of the stomach lining.

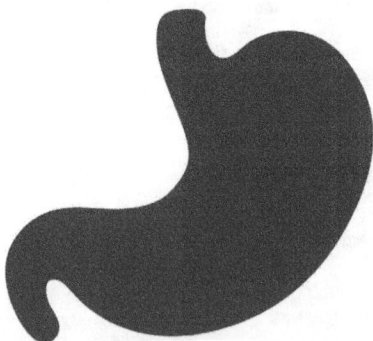

Figure 13: Stomach

Spleen

- Approximately 6 ounces/170 grams.
- Approximately 4 inches long, so about the size of a toilet paper tube.
- Located in the upper left of the abdominal cavity, left of the stomach.
- Recycles red blood cells and stores white blood cells.
- Humans can live without the spleen.
- Simply referred to as the spleen. Examples:
  - Ruptured spleen – a severely injured spleen.
  - Splenomegaly – an enlarged spleen.

Figure 14: Spleen

Small Intestine

- Approximately 20 feet/6 meters long.
- Approximately as wide as one finger.
- Comprised of three sections.
  - Duodenum
  - Jejunum
  - Ileum
- Fills most of the abdominal cavity.
- Conducts 90% of digestion and reabsorbs nutrients.
- Passes the food waste to the large intestine.
- Referred to as the bowels.
- Medical terminology starts with "entero-" or "intestin-". Examples:
  - Enteropathy – a disease of the intestines.
  - Enterospasm – constant contractions of the intestines.

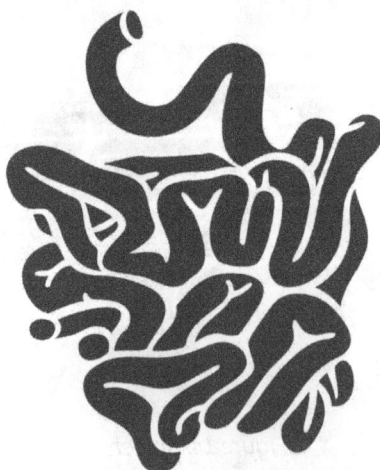

Figure 15: Small Intestine

Large Intestine

- Approximately 5 feet/1.5 meters long.
- Approximately as wide as three fingers.
- Comprised of four sections.
  - Cecum
  - Colon
  - Rectum
  - Anal cavity
- Surrounds the small intestine in the abdominal cavity.
- The appendix is connected to the cecum.
- Absorbs water from the remaining food waste and then ejects the waste from the body as feces.
- Also referred to as the bowels.
- Medical terminology also starts with "entero-" or "intestin-". Examples:
  - Intestinal obstruction – a blocked or twisted section of the intestines that is preventing waste removal.
  - Intestinal cancer – cancer in the intestines. Can be further specified by the intestinal section, such as colon cancer.

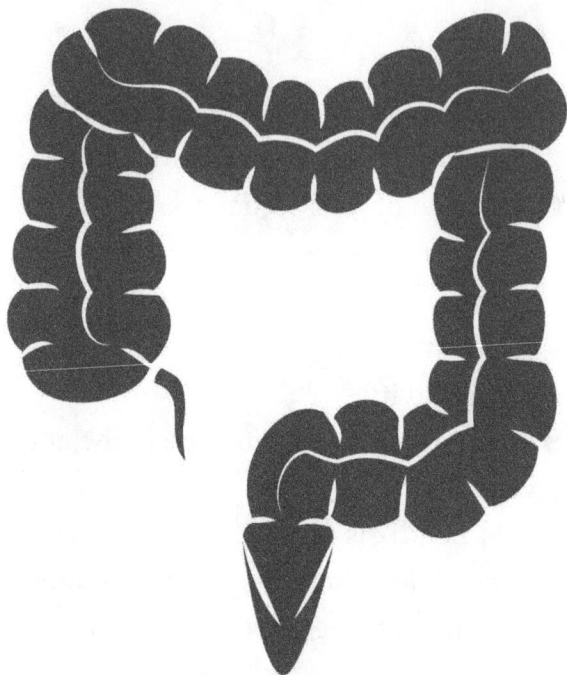

Figure 16: Large Intestine

ACCURACY – Please note that the above list of facts is not all-encompassing. Exceptions exist for different medical wordings, requiring confirmatory research to ensure the correct terminology is used. For example, cirrhosis is a liver disease cited by pathologists that does not start with "hepa-".

Head Dissection

The primary purpose for dissecting the head is to gain access to the final organ, the brain. Brain injuries can reveal why the person died, or can help piece the overall story together.

In the JonBenét Ramsey case, although her death

was actually caused by strangulation, the examination of the head and brain revealed that she had a head injury that caused her head to bleed internally and her brain to swell. The importance of this finding was that it proved there was some sort of violent incident that occurred that night prior to her strangulation.

Some pathologists open the body's head prior to cutting the Y-incision and examining the torso's organs. Every autopsy I've been a part of, however, saved the head for last. There is no required order to the process.

Whenever the head is addressed in the course of the autopsy, the body block is moved from beneath the shoulder blades to the bottom of the head/upper neck in order to lift the head up, while immobilizing it.

The biggest concern pathologists have when opening the head is providing the remains to the next of kin in a condition that still allows for an open-casket viewing. For this reason, pathologists follow very specific methods of cutting into the skull.

First, an incision is cut from one ear around the back of the head to the other ear. Then the pathologist takes hold of the top part of the cut and starts separating the scalp from the skull, using the scalpel and turning the scalp inside out as she goes up the head. She continues this scalping until the entire top of the skull is exposed and the scalp lies inside out over the body's face. Note: the scalp is never removed. The front of the scalp is still connected to the forehead. It's just turned inside out.

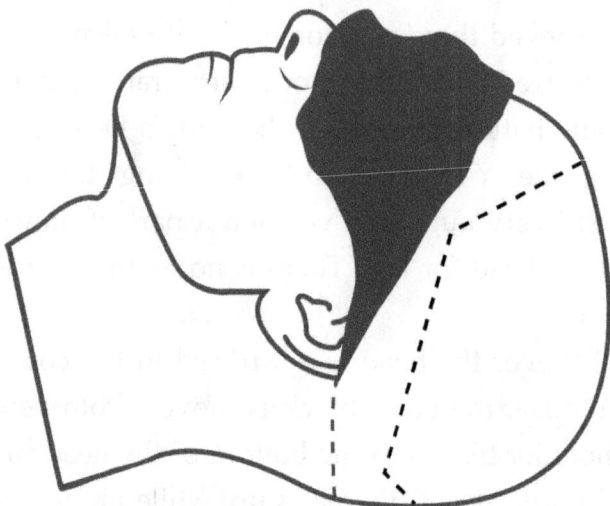

Figure 17: Scalp Over Face with Skull Cap Cut Outlined

The pathologist inspects the outer skull and inner scalp, searching for injuries or breaks. Then a special electric saw, called a bone saw or, more commonly, a **Stryker saw**, is used to cut through the skull.

Figure 18: Stryker Saw

The term "Stryker saw" comes from the fact that one of the primary manufacturers of this device is a company named Stryker. Just as the term "Xerox" became a way to refer to any photocopier, although Xerox is just one company's name, Stryker became a common way to refer to this type of saw. Keep in mind that the rib saw discussed previously in this chapter is also called a bone saw, yet is a very different instrument. So to avoid confusion, most medical professionals just use the terms rib saw and Stryker saw.

> ACCURACY - Keep in mind that two very different types of saws, with different functions, are called bone saws. They are more commonly referred to as rib saws and Stryker saws.

The Stryker saw works not by having a sharp blade, but by vibrating the blade intensely. The vibration is what cuts through the bone, but won't go through soft tissue. The hazard of using these saws is they create a significant cloud of bone dust. For this reason, while everyone interacting with the body already should be properly protected with PPE at all times, when using the Stryker saw, everyone nearby <u>must</u> have on masks and eye protection.

As marked in Figure 17, the cut goes from the top of the skull down to just above the ear, and then around the skull to the back. The cut is the same on both sides of the skull, so that when done, the majority of the skull can be removed as a skull cap. At the very back of the skull, where the cuts from both sides meet, the pathologist cuts out a pointed notch in the skull. This notch becomes very important when putting the skull back together.

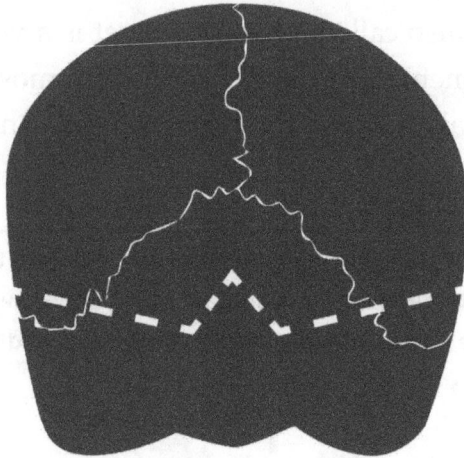

Figure 19: Back-of-Skull Notch

Once the pathologist removes the skull cap, the brain is exposed and can also be removed for examination.

Brain

- Approximately 3 pounds/1.5 kilograms.
- Approximately the size of a Cornish hen.
- The brain has three regions.
    - Brainstem
    - Cerebellum

- ○ Cerebrum
- The cerebrum is the main part of the brain and has four areas.
  - ○ Frontal lobe (front part, near the forehead).
  - ○ Parietal lobe (top part).
  - ○ Temporal lobe (bottom part).
  - ○ Occipital lobe (back part).
- Medical terminology starts with "encephal-" or "cerebr-". Examples:
  - ○ Encephalitis – the inflammation of the brain.
  - ○ Encephalomalacia – the softening or loss of brain tissue, normally from infection.
  - ○ Cerebral palsy – literally means brain paralysis, and refers to a brain injury or underdevelopment that prevents free, controlled motor functions.
  - ○ Cerebral infarction – a stroke. Blood blockage prevents circulation to the brain.

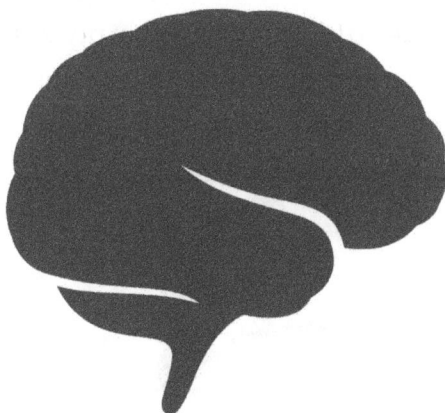

Figure 20: Brain

Closing Up

After the internal examination, the pathologist must prepare the body so that it can be released. To do this, she must sew up the major cuts (the Y-incision and the back of the head). First she puts all of the organs and the breastbone/ribs into a heavy-duty, leak-proof plastic bag, brain included. She ties that bag shut and then puts it into the empty chest cavity. She then sews the Y-incision closed.

> PROCEDURE – By placing all of the organs into the organ bag and sewing it inside the body, the pathologist honors all religious requirements, as she is providing the next of kin with the entirety of the remains, allowing their loved one to be buried all in one place.

Pathologists use a specially curved, strong industrial needle and reinforced thick twine to sew the cuts closed. The needle, commonly called an **autopsy needle** but also referred to as a Hadgedorn needle or a sailmaker's needle, curves up sharply at the tip. This way, when the needle is pushed into the skin, which requires a bit of force, it always curves its direction upward, and therefore back out.

Figure 21: Types of Autopsy Needles

To put the head back together, that notch the pathologist cut into the back of the skull becomes very important. The pathologist takes the skull cap and puts it back on the empty skull (remember, the brain is now in the organ bag inside the chest cavity). The notch serves to set the skull cap back into its perfect place, and also helps to keep it there.

Once the skull cap is in place, the pathologist pulls the scalp back from the face, fitting it back into its natural position. The properly set scalp holds the skull cap in place and allows the pathologist to sew everything together by closing the cut at the back of the head. Just as with the Y-incision, she uses the curved autopsy needle and reinforced twine and sews the ear-to-ear cut shut.

When the body leaves the pathologist's care, the only visible evidence of the autopsy will be the sewn Y-incision, which will be covered by clothing, and the sewn cut at the back of the head, which will be hidden by the casket's pillow. So, although the body has been taken all apart, it is still viewable for an open-casket funeral.

Once the pathologist releases the body, it is transported to the appropriate mortician, as identified by the next of kin. The mortician will either prepare the body for funeral by embalming it, or make the necessary arrangements to have it cremated. The embalmed body or the body's ashes are then released to the funeral director so that the remains are accessible to the next of kin. To leave the morgue, the body <u>must</u> be released to a certified mortician.

Lab Work

Toxicology

As I mentioned above, toxicology is the study of chemical substances and their effects on the human body. In the setting of autopsies, toxicologists search for poisons and drugs in the remains. Toxicology testing, also called a **tox screen**, is done at a laboratory by forensic chemists. So at the end of the autopsy, the pathologist labels all of the samples she collected for the tox screen during the autopsy and sends them to the lab.

PROCEDURE – During the autopsy, the pathologist collects samples from each of the organs, as well as blood, bile, urine, and the vitreous humor for toxicological testing. These samples are stored individually and labeled accordingly before being sent to the lab.

The toxicology process takes a long time, sometimes months, and is the main reason final autopsy reports are so delayed. The autopsy cannot be considered complete until all of the lab results have been reported. There are several reasons why the tox screenings take so long:

- Each organ and fluid sample must be tested individually.
- Each sample is first tested by a preliminary test, which is merely indicative, not accurate proof, of a toxin's presence, but goes relatively quickly.
- If a preliminary test's result is positive, then a much more time-consuming confirmatory test is performed. This test is very specific and can tell which substances are present and in what dosage.
- There is typically a backlog at laboratories due to the volume of samples waiting to be tested. Each new case must wait its turn.

As with the autopsy itself, the pathologist can put a rush on certain toxicology requests in order to bump that testing up in the long line of samples preceding it. The pathologist will have to specifically explain why this case is more important than all of the other cases that have been waiting.

It's important to keep in mind that not every poison or drug known to man is tested in a typical tox screen. The normal screening tests only for those drugs most often used/encountered. The time required to test for everything is far too great, and each test costs the lab money. If the pathologist, based on either the autopsy or law enforcement reports on the investigation, has indication that a drug or poison may be present that is not typically tested for, she need only add that specific drug to the request and the toxicologists will add it to their screens.

> **PROCEDURE –** The typical tox screen does not test for every drug. Therefore, a negative screening does not mean there are no drugs present, just not the ones tested for.

The drugs typically included on the normal tox screen include marijuana, alcohol, opiates, psychostimulants, and barbiturates. The common toxins often tested for in normal tox screens are arsenic and heavy metals.

Histology

Sometimes the cause of death is not visible to the naked eye and can only be discovered by the microscopic analysis of the deceased's organs. That's where the histology tests come into play. **Histology** is the study of microscopic anatomy. Histotechnicians study the tissues at the microscopic level searching for abnormalities, often indicating disease.

Just as with toxicology, the samples the pathologist collected for histology must be individually stored and adequately labeled. These samples are then sent to the histology lab.

> **PROCEDURE –** The samples kept for microscopic study are tissue samples, so are taken only from the organs.

Most coroner and medical examiner offices have their own histology labs on premises. But, if not, the samples are sent to a predetermined laboratory. The histology results do not take nearly as long as the toxicology reports do.

Autopsy Report

The autopsy is not considered complete until the pathologist issues a final autopsy report. For it to be thorough, she needs to consider everything from all angles before she settles on a cause, manner, and mechanism of death. This means she must wait for the lab results to be completed before coming to a final conclusion.

She can also take law enforcement reports, previous medical histories, where and how the body was found, reports on the deceased's actions prior to death, and a host of other nonmedical information into account while forming her opinion.

The autopsy report will include the cause and manner of death, a time-of-death estimation, all personal information, and any and all artifacts noted during the autopsy, including all injuries, whether or not they contributed to the death.

Issuing the autopsy report is the pathologist's final action for each case, and closes the autopsy for that office. Law enforcement investigators take the autopsy report findings as an official addition to their investigation.

Case Study 2: Beverley Allitt – False Angel

Beverley Allitt was a twenty-two-year-old pediatric nurse at the Grantham and Kesteven Hospital, Lincolnshire, England, for three months. During her time there, she was the cause of extreme medical conditions in thirteen children which were not related to any of their initial diagnoses. Four of the children died. She is considered a serial killer and was labeled the "Angel of Death" by the media.

In early childhood, Beverley apparently suffered from a mental disorder that exhibited itself as an extreme need for attention. She would frequent medical facilities claiming a variety of illnesses and was known to often wear bandages and casts for nonexistent injuries.

Her behavior continued into adulthood. She enrolled in nurse training, where she continued claiming false illnesses and once purported to be pregnant, although tests proved otherwise. She engaged in deeply concerning activities, such as wiping feces on nursing home walls. In training, she continually failed her exams.

Despite this, in February 1991, she was accepted for a temporary position in the Grantham and Kesteven Hospital. This was supposed to be a six-month internship, but the hospital was critically understaffed. The pediatric section, Ward 4, only had three full-time nurses to provide twenty-four-hour care for their tiny patients. Beverley was assigned to assist Ward 4, and opting not to do any sort of background check due to their staffing issues, the hospital quickly promoted her out of her internship to the position of children's nurse, citing her willingness to console parents and take on extra shifts.

On February 21 1991, two days after Beverley started working there, seven-month-old Liam Taylor was admitted to Ward 4 due to a chest infection associated with the flu. That night, under Beverley's care, Liam took a concerning turn for the worse and stopped breathing. The doctors were able to stabilize him, and Beverley was specifically assigned to him as a "specialing" attendant, which simply means she was given the duty of one-to-one nursing and checking on him. She volunteered for extra duty that night to stay with him.

In the early morning hours, Liam had a second respiratory emergency. Beverley was the one who raised the alarm, and based on her story and the time it took to resuscitate him, doctors estimated Liam had not been breathing on his own for over an hour. The nursing staff was very concerned that the monitors had not sounded the alarm and praised Beverley for doing so herself.

During the resuscitation efforts, Liam suffered cardiac arrest and was kept alive only with the aid of life-support machines. His parents decided to remove life support and he died. The doctors called the cause of death heart failure, which was very different from the chest infection he was admitted for.

On March 5, eleven-year-old Timothy Hardwick, who suffered from cerebral palsy, was admitted to Ward 4 after an epileptic seizure. Beverley was assigned as his specialing attendant. Once again, after checking in on him alone, Beverley shouted out for his doctors. Timothy was not breathing. The doctors could not resuscitate him and he died. Timothy's death was blamed on his epilepsy.

Doctors had been treating one-year-old Kayley Desmond for several days for a chest infection. She had been admitted to Ward 4 on March 3, and was recovering well. On March 8, Kayley went into cardiac arrest. The doctors were able to resuscitate her. A thorough examination led to the discovery of a puncture mark under her armpit with an air bubble in it. The doctors surmised it must have been from an accidental injection during the resuscitation efforts. Kayley was transferred to the Queens Medical Center in Nottingham, where she recovered.

On March 20, five-month-old Paul Crampton was admitted to Ward 4 for simple observation after a mild chest infection.

On March 21, five-year-old Bradley Gibson was admitted for pneumonia. Soon after his IV was administered, he stopped breathing. Doctors were able to resuscitate him, but later that night he experienced a myocardial infarction (heart attack). Beverley was once again working a voluntary extra night shift. The doctors transferred Bradley to the Queens Medical Center, where he recovered.

On March 22, two-year-old Yik Hung Chan was admitted because a fall had fractured his skull. He, too, stopped breathing, and he was also transferred to Nottingham, where he recovered. The doctors attributed his symptoms to his injuries.

On March 23, doctors had just finished telling Paul Crampton's family they were starting discharging procedures when Beverley once again yelled for help. Doctors described Paul's sudden critical condition as circulatory shock with labored breathing. Paul recovered, but doctors told the family they now wanted to keep him longer. The next day, March 24, Paul's mysterious symptoms returned, and although it took much longer, he again eventually recovered.

Beverley did not return to the hospital for the next three days because she had scheduled time off.

During this time, Paul's condition greatly improved and he had no further episodes. When Beverley returned on March 28, however, so did Paul's mysterious symptoms. For a third time, Paul recovered, but this time his attending physician, Dr. Nelson Porter, ordered that he be transferred to the Queens Medical Center for specialized treatment. Beverley volunteered to accompany Paul's mother in the transporting ambulance. Dr. Porter took several blood samples before releasing Paul. Paul eventually made a full recovery and was sent home. The blood samples were critically low in sugar. Doctors did not know what to make of Paul's sudden and severe hypoglycemic episodes.

On April 1, two-month-old twins, Becky and Katie Phillips were transferred to Ward 4 for observation. They had been seen for a nonspecific illness blamed on their premature birth. The doctors quickly released the twins to their parents to take home. Within a couple of hours of being home, however, Becky started convulsing. When she was returned to the hospital, she was pronounced dead on arrival. The doctors urged the Phillipses to readmit Katie, who had no signs of any ailment, for observation due to Becky's death.

On April 5, Katie, too, became gravely ill and stopped breathing. The doctors revived her, but two days later she suffered another attack. Again she was revived, and this time she was transferred to Nottingham, where doctors noted her lungs were collapsed, she had several broken ribs, and she had severe brain damage because of lack of oxygen. The collapsed lungs and broken ribs were attributed to the resuscitation efforts.

The twins' mother, sadly, was so moved by Beverley's attentiveness and apparent concern that she asked Beverley to be Katie's godmother.

On April 7, six-year-old Michael Davidson was transferred to Ward 4 after a successful surgery. He had been accidentally shot in the chest by an air pellet, and had no illness. On April 9, Michael mysteriously collapsed and stopped breathing. The doctors were able to revive Michael, but could not find anything associated with his injury or surgery that would cause him to stop breathing. Once he was stabilized, Michael was once again placed under Beverley's care. Later that night, he again stopped breathing. The doctors were able to save him a second time, and he eventually fully recovered.

On April 13, eight-month-old Christopher Peasgood was admitted to Ward 4 with a chest infection. In what was finally revealing itself to be a pattern to the attending doctors, his condition unexpectedly worsened to the point of not breathing. Upon resuscitation, Christopher Peasgood was transferred to the Queens Medical Center and eventually recovered.

Two days later, on April 15, nine-month-old Christopher King, who was being held due to a severe stomach flu, also stopped breathing. He, as well, was transferred to Nottingham and also recovered.

On April 18, seven-week-old Patrick Elstone stopped breathing. Patrick had been admitted to Ward 4 due to an ear infection, and had no respiratory issues. The doctors resuscitated and stabilized Patrick, but later that night Beverley again raised the alarm that Patrick had once again stopped breathing. After he was revived this second time, the doctors transferred Patrick to the Intensive Care Unit, where he was determined to have suffered severe brain damage, most likely due to lack of oxygen.

The doctors were greatly concerned about the number of severe cases happening on the ward, especially when most were admitted with unrelated diagnoses. They feared the ward housed an unidentified airborne virus.

Beverley's final victim, 15-month-old Claire Peck, was admitted to the ward on April 21 for a severe asthma attack. As with the other children, it was Beverley who sounded the alarm that Claire had stopped breathing. The doctors revived Claire and stabilized her. Mere minutes later, Beverley called out that Claire was crashing again. Claire suffered a heart attack, and the doctors could not revive her a second time.

The hospital ordered a clinical autopsy of Claire, but the pathologist ruled her death as natural. Dr. Porter, frustrated and perplexed over the number of incidents, officially requested an internal inquiry. He asked for a second autopsy and made a call to the police. He then set up strict rules for the nurses to follow in regards to administering any medication.

The hospital initially denied the second autopsy, until Dr. Porter ran extensive tests on Claire's blood and reported unusually high levels of potassium. The hospital ordered the exhumation of Claire's body. The second autopsy revealed the presence of Lignocaine, a powerful drug used for cardiac arrest victims, but never ordered to treat a child.

Armed with this finding, the police started a full investigation of the ward. They discovered that a key to the medicine refrigerator was missing. They also reviewed each of the suspicious cases and charted out when each child was in the ward. Heightening their concerns, several pages of the nurses' time log were missing. With the logs they had, though, investigators soon discovered that the only nurse or doctor who was working every time a child experienced a critical episode was Beverley Allitt.

A background check revealed Beverley's unusual behavioral history, and proved she was unqualified to serve in her position. In a search of Beverley's home, police found torn parts of the missing time logs.

Beverley was charged on July 26, 1991. During the arrest and trial, she maintained her innocence.

Beverley once again began claiming a variety of odd illnesses, which resulted in several delays of her trial. She actually lost a significant amount of weight during her incarceration, which many believe was her attempt to validate ailments.

All of the blood available for the thirteen victims was tested and consistently showed excessively high levels of insulin and potassium. Insulin was kept in the ward's refrigerator with the missing key. When a person has an insulin overdose, the blood sugar drops dramatically. Without sugar, the body's cells can't function. This hypoglycemia causes the body to break down, and often the victim stops breathing.

For the thirteen victims, Beverley was charged with four counts of murder, eleven counts of attempted murder, and eleven counts of causing grievous bodily harm. She pled not guilty. On May 28 1993, Beverley was found guilty on all counts and was sentenced to thirteen consecutive life sentences, without any possibility for parole. Because of her strange behavior and need for attention, she was ordered to serve out her sentence at the Rampton Secure Hospital, in Nottinghamshire, England, which is a high-security psychiatric hospital. Many of the victims' parents feel life at this particular psychiatric hospital is not punishment enough for her crimes.

Beverley eventually admitted to three of the murders and six of the assaults.

Had it not been for Dr. Porter requesting a second autopsy, foul play may never have been a consideration for all of these victims. Toxicology during the second autopsy revealed a drug that could not have been used on a child for any reason other than to intend harm, opening the entire situation up to a criminal investigation and the eventual capture of a murderer.

Chapter 5: Decomposition

I would be remiss in my discussion about death if I neglected to include the topic of decomposition. What naturally happens to a body after death is important to any author writing about remains in any capacity. Why are the zombies on *The Walking Dead* portrayed as slimy and green, while the monsters in mummy movies as brittle and brown? When the protagonist stumbles upon a body two days after death, should it still be pristine? What happens as a body decomposes? Why does decay occur and what affects it? An understanding of decomposition, while not the most savory of topics, is essential when seeking realism for your bodies.

The physiology of the human body is an amazing network of systems interwoven to maintain the body's **homeostasis**, which is an internal equilibrium despite continual environmental variables. Decomposition begins at the moment of death, when the internal systems cease to function and internal stability adjusts to the surrounding conditions.

> **TERMS – Homeostasis is the body's physiology working to keep an internal stability against constantly changing external environmental factors.**

Much of our knowledge of decomposition was discovered at special research facilities called **body farms**, where cadavers are studied under a host of variable conditions.

Renowned anthropologist, Dr. William Bass, established the first and most significant body farm in 1981, at the University of Tennessee Medical Center in Knoxville, Tennessee. Dr. Bass stored several bodies at various levels of exposures to chart the decomposition process during environmental variables. Over a hundred volunteers allocate their bodies each year to the body farm through a donation process finalized prior to death. Several other body farms have been established since, and in 2017 the Northern Michigan University campus opened the first cold-weather body farm in Marquette, Michigan.

Environmental Variables

If anything can be learned about decomposition, it's that any change in environmental conditions can affect the type and rate of decay, which we'll discuss throughout this chapter. Higher temperatures tend to accelerate decomposition, while cooler temperatures slow it down. Wetter environments create artifacts on the body not seen in dryer areas. If the body is protected by clothing or otherwise safeguarded in some way from the elements, decomposition timeframes change.

With that in mind, as we progress through this chapter, I'm going to provide a timeline for each process. Take each timeframe with great reservations, however, as the exceptions can vary the timing of each stage significantly.

On that same note, with a few very specific exceptions – which we'll cover in the next chapter – the susceptibility of decomposition to environmental changes makes any reliable estimation of when a person died nearly impossible. Time-of-death windows cannot be established solely from the decomposition stage of remains.

It's time for us to put the gross into anatomy!

Autolysis and Putrefaction

Why does decomposition happen? What is behind the decay? There are two primary processes of decomposition: **autolysis** and **putrefaction**. Autolysis occurs when the body's enzymes begin breaking down its own tissues, while in putrefaction, it's bacteria that breaks down the tissues. Both of these activities create gases, which cause the body to bloat, float in water, and have a foul odor.

Timeline: Immediate

Autolysis literally means "self-digestion." Human

cells contain digestive enzymes called **lysosomes**. These enzymes are instrumental in digesting and recycling organic material within each cell. At the time of death, when the body can no longer maintain the cells' homeostasis, the lysosomes escape and begin digesting (breaking down) the tissues within the body.

> **TERMS – Autolysis is a form of decomposition in which the body is broken down by its own enzymes.**

As with autolysis, putrefaction occurs immediately after death. Mainly found in the large intestine, hundreds of types of helpful bacteria, numbering in the trillions, assist the digestive system in eliminating waste from the body. At death, once the body stops providing their meals, the bacteria begin consuming the body itself.

> **TERMS – Putrefaction is the decomposition of the body due to bacterial activity.**

As the bacteria digest the tissues of the body, their waste is no longer combined and expelled with the human's excrement. This collection of waste turns that area of the body a greenish-black color. The outward visualization of putrefaction first manifests near the body's inner right hip, which, anatomically speaking, is where the large intestine, and therefore this bacteria, is closest to the skin's surface.

Timeline: 1 – 3 Days

With blood no longer taking up the cardiovascular system, the bacteria use the veins and arteries as passageways throughout the body, marking their progress with the same discoloration. The veins and arteries are discolored as well, creating visible black lines throughout the body. This stage of decomposition is called **marbling**. In paranormal fiction, marbling's blackened veins are often described to indicate the creature is undead.

> **TERMS – Marbling is the stage of decomposition in which the circulatory system is dyed a dark greenish-black color due to the putrefaction process.**

As putrefaction progresses, the bacteria's gasses get trapped within the body. This causes the abdomen and male genitalia to bloat.

Timeline: 5 – 9 Days

In normal conditions after five to nine days, the swelling will continue to the neck and face, often forcing the eyes to bulge and the tongue to stick out.

> **FUN FACT – Because putrefaction gases begin collecting in the large intestine, bodies found in water typically float from the hip area, with the face, shoulders, and legs submerged.**

During this same time period, the gas stretches the body to the point that the skin starts to blister. The outer layer of the skin, the epidermis, begins to tear and actually disconnects from the lower layers. This action is the **skin slippage** I touched on in Chapter 2 when discussing various difficulties with fingerprinting a cadaver.

Skin slippage results in large areas of the outer skin falling off of the body. The under layers of skin that become exposed are quite red, sometimes leading laypersons to conclude an injury occurred, such as an abrasion or burn, when in reality no injury is present at all.

Timeline: 2 Weeks

After a couple weeks, the internal pressure from the putrefaction gases is so great that it forces any remaining urine and feces out of the body. It also drives any food left in the stomach up the esophagus and out of the mouth. At this time the food is digested to the point that it is a dark liquid, which can lead anyone finding the body to believe there is injury around the nose and mouth, although there is not.

The internal organs begin to liquefy around this timeframe, depending on what sort of membrane surrounds them and whether the organ is one with a higher muscle content. Sometimes the membrane will hold the liquid in for a time, acting as a sort of organic "water balloon." Eventually the membranes, too, will break down and the liquefied organs will also be forced out of the nose and mouth. The gases are so intense at this stage that they often mix with the liquid, creating a foam seen around the various orifices.

Timeline: 3 – 4 Weeks

In the ideal environment, at around three to four weeks, the deceased's skin blackens. The face continues to bloat, and with the discoloration, visual identification becomes nearly impossible. Because the skin becomes an obsidian-black, even race is difficult to determine. The body is so bloated at this time that a visual inspection often gives the impression that the individual was obese, even if the person was incredibly slim just prior to death.

As mentioned above, temperatures greatly affect the rate at which decomposition occurs, and a medical examiner would never use the decomposition stage to make a time-of-death ruling. A body in hot temperatures will rapidly progress through the stages, while a body in colder temperatures can be preserved for much longer. This is why morgues keep the bodies in a refrigerated room until it is time for the autopsy.

> ACCURACY – Fingernails, toenails, and hair do not continue to grow after death, as the old wives' tale suggests. As the skin dries, it contracts around them, making it appear as though they've grown.

Saponification

Saponification only happens in wet environments. It's a bit technical, but I'll try to avoid an all-out chemistry lesson. **Saponification** is a chemical reaction in which water converts a fat into a soap. In bodies, the fats are fatty acids and the soap they are converted into is a white or gray substance called **adipocere**.

Timeline: 5 – 9 Days

The saponification process needs warmer temperatures, wet environments, and the presence of fatty acids. Decomposition must create skin slippage before the fatty acids are exposed to the damp environment. At that point, the saponification processes begins and continues at a rate dependent on how warm the surrounding area is.

> TERMS – Adipocere is a waxy substance found on dead human and animal bodies located in extremely damp areas or under water.

As the adipocere covers the body, it begins to protect it by acting as a preservative and greatly slows the decomposition process.

While adipocere is common in all extremely damp external environments, it has also been documented on bodies found submerged in bathtubs. Depending on the environment, adipocere can develop as early as two weeks or as late as several months after death.

Mummification

Most people associate "mummification" with pharaohs, pyramid tombs, and the monster movies they inspire. Historically, a mummy was created through an elaborate embalming process referred to as mummification. However, "mummification" is also used to describe a stage of natural decomposition, as long as specific conditions exist. In decomposition, **mummification** occurs when the tissues of the body dry out. As it dries, the skin becomes extremely delicate, tearing easily, and takes on a dull brown color.

> ACCURACY: Mummification can stand for a process of embalming used in Ancient Egypt, or for a natural stage of decomposition in arid environments. They are distinct from each other and should not be confused.

Timeline: 2 – 36 Months

A body mummifies in extremely dry, very warm environments, such as deserts, which makes sense when we consider how many remains were mummified in Ancient Egypt. This arid climate contributes to a rapid evaporation of the body's fluids. This process can also happen indoors in other areas of the world if the room is significantly dehumidified. Mummification has been found in bodies lying extremely close to a room's radiator or heater, for example.

How quickly a body mummifies relies completely on how arid the environment is. The quicker the body's moisture evaporates, the quicker it stops the process of decomposition. Once a body is completely dried out, it is preserved in that state.

The drying process kills the bacteria within the body and therefore acts as a preservative for the remains, making postmortem evaluation easier. Mummified bodies can maintain their condition for decades or longer if dried completely.

Wounds deeper than the outer layers of the skin are petrified and protected. Autopsies of mummified remains, however, are precarious because the dehydration lends itself to disintegration as opposed to clean cuts. Most autopsy attempts must first endeavor to rehydrate the body through the tissue-building process we covered in Chapter 2 in the discussion of postmortem fingerprinting.

Bog Bodies

Often erroneously referred to as mummification because it is also preserved, a bog body undergoes a completely different process, similar to pickling. The preservation in these situations is a biochemical reaction that stops decomposition. These bodies are typically found in cooler, wetter environments, conditions opposite those required for natural mummification. These chemical reactions occur because of the peat (dead plant material) and the highly acidic water present in the bogs.

> ACCURACY: Mummification and bog bodies are completely different processes. In natural mummification, the preservation is a result of the dehydration of the body, while in bogs, a biochemical reaction pickles the body.

The pickling effect works quicker the colder the temperature. Many anthropologists believe this is because in cold weather, the natural bacteria that initiate decomposition are not active. Because the bodies are so well preserved, a timeline on how long the pickling takes has not been officially established. Many anthropologists have a hard time determining how long a body has been in the bog because of how well persevered all bog bodies are. Of particular note, once the remains are removed from the bog's conditions, decomposition resumes, often at an accelerated rate.

Skeletonization

The absolute final stage of decomposition is called **skeletonization**, which is when none of the body's soft tissue remain and nothing is left of the body but the bones.

Timeline: 1.5 – 10 Years

The timing of skeletonization varies widely. Studies at the body farm found bodies that had been buried, and therefore protected from environmental changes, could take up to a decade to reach full skeletonization. Bodies in water, however, could reach this stage in a couple of years, assuming no fish are feeding on it, which would accelerate the process. A body in the open air, exposed to the elements, can reach skeletonization in a year and a half. Again, this is assuming the conditions are not extreme and that there is no insect or animal activity, which is not terribly realistic.

As you can see, the rate and type of decomposition are as varied as the many types of environments bodies can be in. It's impossible to do any sort of accurate time-of-death estimation just based on a decomposition stage, with a few exceptions. Those exceptions, as well as the other official time-of-death estimate methods, are the topic of the next chapter.

Chapter 6: Time-of-Death Determinations

I decided to break this topic out into its own chapter because it covers one of my biggest pet peeves with fictional portrayals of death – time-of-death estimations. How many times have you been enjoying a good story when the coroner, medical examiner, random doctor, or even the investigator proclaims, "I'd wager the time of death is somewhere between noon and 12:15, give or take"? In real life, that *never* happens! In this chapter, I'm going to break down the various methods used to estimate a time of death, and show you how it is never to the minute, and rarely to the hour.

> ACCURACY – Time-of-death approximates are never to the minute. The estimated window of time in which the death occurred is typically no less than 12 hours, and is often days, weeks, and sometimes months long.

The official term for time-of-death estimates is the **postmortem interval (PMI)** . That is the window of time the pathologist sets during which the death most probably occurred. There are a variety of methods the pathologist can use and take into account when determining this window. However, as you'll see in the discussion below, none of the methods have a very reliable accuracy because there are too many variables to take into account. In the real world, the essential data needed to address each of those variables are difficult, and often impossible, to obtain.

> TERMS – The postmortem interval (PMI) is the official term for the window of time the pathologist estimates the death occurred in. In practice, most professionals just say "time of death."

Witness Window

The most basic, and most obvious, time-of-death window is the time between the last reported instance the deceased was seen alive and when the deceased's body was discovered. This requires interviews to map out the deceased's actions prior to his death, but that is standard procedure in any death investigation.

If the deceased's neighbor was the last person to see him alive as he stumbled home drunk on Wednesday night at 10:45, and the deceased's housekeeper discovered his body when she arrived at 10:30 on Thursday morning, we know the death happened in that twelve-hour period.

Sometimes this standard window can be very helpful, especially if it's only a few hours long.

However, if the deceased has been missing for over a month, the window, while significant, is too big. For this reason, pathologists use a variety of other time-lapse indicators to narrow their estimates.

> **PROCEDURE** – The witness window can be very helpful in PMI estimations if it provides a short timeframe, however, for periods that extend to days or weeks, the window gets too large.

Keep in mind that the "witness" in the witness window does not have to be a human being. The last time the deceased was captured on video can also establish the time-of-death window.

Sometimes documents can act as the witness. For example, if the deceased has a fast-food receipt in his possession that has a time and date stamp on it, investigators can use that to establish the last time the person was alive.

The only instance when any PMI is truly specific is when the death itself was actually witnessed. If Rayna saw Tere shoot Elle at 11:15 AM, then we know exactly when the death occurred. Without an eyewitness or a video capturing the event, any other time-of-death estimate cannot be this specific.

Decompositional Changes

As we discussed in the last chapter, the body undergoes many changes after death due to decomposition.

However, because of so many variables that can speed up, slow down, or even change the type of decomposition, it's hard to use it as a time-of-death indicator. In the case of advanced decomposition, the variables make estimating a PMI almost impossible.

However, there are several early decompositional changes that can provide a time-of-death window. As with every other method we will discuss in this chapter, keep in mind that any estimate has a pretty significant margin of error percentage, and makes any determination no more than an educated guess.

Livor Mortis

While the human body is alive, the heart pumps to create blood pressure, which is the force that moves the blood throughout the entire body. Once the heart stops pumping, the blood stops flowing. This is why a postmortem wound looks different from an ante-mortem wound.

When the blood pressure is no longer present to keep the blood going where it needs to go, the blood begins to seep out of the blood vessels; the veins, arteries, and capillaries. As is the case with any liquid, the blood will move downward in the body, pulled by gravity. When I say downward, I don't necessarily mean to the toes. I mean to the part of the body that is closest to the ground. So if a body is lying on its back, the blood will be pulled to the back of the legs, back of the arms, and back of the torso. If the body is laying on its front, the blood will pool at the front of the legs, arms, and torso. If the body is found slumped in a seated position in a chair, the blood will pool at the feet and butt. My point is, no matter how the body is positioned at death, gravity will pull the blood down to the lowest-lying areas.

Once the blood settles in the gravity-dependent areas of the body, it begins to stain the skin. This staining is called **livor mortis** or **lividity**. Both terms are used interchangeably in the profession. The stain is typically reddish, much like a sunburn, but can also be a darker blue to purple. It can be difficult to see in people of color or in cases of advanced decomposition where the skin has darkened. When set, the stain is permanent.

> **TERMS –** Livor mortis, or lividity, is a permanent red to blueish-purple staining of the skin in a dead person caused from the pooling of blood by gravity in that area.

The staining does not occur in areas where the skin is supported by tight-fitting clothing, such as a bra strap or belt, or where it's laying on top of an object, such as when a body's torso is laying on one of the arms. This protection against lividity staining is called **blanching**.

Humor me for a second for a quick exercise. (Audience participation – yay!) Turn one of your hands palm up. With a finger from the other hand, press down on the meaty area just below your thumb. Do you see how, when you lift your finger, that area (in the shape of your finger) is a much lighter color for a second or two? That is blanching at work. You are pressing the blood out of that area of skin, and it is much paler until the blood rushes back in. The same exact thing happens with lividity. If a woman was wearing a bra and was lying on her back after she died, although lividity is occurring on her entire back, the bra strap pushes the blood out of that section of skin. So that area does not stain. So, just like your sunglasses leave unburned, pale circles around your eyes after your face has been sunburned, that bra strap leaves a pale image of itself in the lividity on the body. In the case of the body lying on its arm, there is a pale stripe across the torso free from lividity that matches the shape of the arm.

The blood starts to seep out of its vessels and pool as soon as the blood pressure ceases, which is immediately after death. However, for the blood to actually start staining, it takes at least two hours. The staining process continues until lividity is set, normally at around twelve hours after death, but that can vary dramatically based on different environmental conditions, such as temperature or body position.

Once the lividity is set, it is set, so after that timeframe, there is no way to determine how long the body has been there just by livor mortis. The lividity would be the same for twelve hours and forty-eight hours. Trying to determine the rate of lividity to come up with a time of death prior to the twelve hours is almost impossible.

PROCEDURE – The most lividity can tell a pathologist as far as PMI is concerned is that the body has been dead for at least twelve hours, but that's not overly specific as it could have been dead for days.

Lividity is extremely helpful in another area of death investigations: determining whether a body was moved after death. We know that livor mortis occurs in the gravity-dependent areas of the body. With that as a given, if the coroner/ME arrives at a death scene and finds lividity on the decedent's back, yet the body is laying facedown, that body has been moved. On this planet, it is impossible for blood to pool upwards and stain areas of skin that oppose gravity. In these situations, investigators know that the body was moved after lividity was set, which means there is someone who needs to be located and interviewed, be it suspect, witness, or responding police officer.

If the body is moved before the twelve-hour (give or take) window required to set lividity, it is possible to have two lividity patterns on the body. For example, when Paul killed John, John fell onto his back. Lividity started and the skin on John's back began to stain. Four hours later, Paul came back to try to clean the scene so no one would know he was present at John's death. Paul rolled John's body over to clean up any evidence that may have been below him. At that point the blood that had pooled on John's back gets pulled by gravity to John's front, but his back had already started staining. The blood then stains John's front until it is fully set. When the coroner/ME arrives, John's body now has two lividity stains: one on his front, which makes sense as he was found facedown, but also one on his back, which is impossible as it flows against gravity. Anytime a body has more than one lividity stain, that body has been moved.

Rigor Mortis

Another change to the body in early decomposition used in PMI determinations is rigor mortis. To fully understand this process requires a knowledge of some specific biology and chemistry. I'll try to boil it down to the essentials for this text.

So, our muscle cells produce a fuel molecule called adenosine triphosphate (ATP). Without going too far into what that is, one of its functions is to act as a lubricant between two fibers in our skeletal muscles, actin and myosin. Fully ATP-lubricated muscles permit the actin and myosin to slide freely against each other, allowing your muscles to contract, enabling you to move.

Has anyone done a workout and then couldn't extend your arms fully the next day? Well, that's because of all the ATP you expelled during your reps. While the ATP levels are depleted, your actin and myosin cannot slide freely. Everyone still with me?

Once a person dies, the body stops producing ATP. With no lubricant, the actin and myosin not only stop sliding freely, but they actually bind together in a biochemical reaction. As a result, the muscles seize in place and become unmovable.

This stiffening of the muscles is called **rigor mortis**, also referred to simply as **rigor**, and is not permanent. Eventually, decomposition will break the bond between the actin and myosin and the muscles will move freely again.

> TERMS – Rigor mortis is the temporary stiffening of the muscles to the point that they will not move.

Rigor mortis is not muscle contractions. The muscles do not move after death, they simply freeze in place. So, for example, if a dead person was sitting on the floor propped up against the wall so that his body formed an "L" (the torso up against the wall and the legs straight out along the floor), when the coroner or medical examiner arrives on the scene and transfers the body to his back, his legs would defy gravity and stick straight up in the air, maintaining the "L" position.

Rigor mortis goes through three phases: the stage when the muscles are setting (the actin and myosin are forming their bond), the stage when the muscles are set (unmovable), and the stage when the muscles release (the actin-myosin bond breaks down).

At its most basic, PMI determinations are based on what's called the **Rule of 8s**. This means the first eight hours after death is stage one, the muscles are setting. The next eight hours form the second stage where the rigor mortis is set. In the third stage, the final eight hours, the muscles release, meaning this entire process should last about twenty-four hours. The Rule of 8s is very rudimentary, however, and many times the entire rigor mortis cycle can take as long as thirty-six hours.

As with livor mortis, once the cycle has completed, there is very little the pathologist can gain from it, except to say the body has been dead for longer than thirty-six hours. The muscles move just as freely at six days after death as they do at the thirty-six hour point.

PROCEDURE – For PMI determinations, the setting stage of rigor mortis lasts from eight to twelve hours, rigor is set for the next eight to twelve hours, and it releases over another eight to twelve hours. The entire cycle can be twenty-four to thirty-six hours. After rigor mortis has released, it cannot give specific timeframes for how long the body's been dead.

Several factors can affect the timing of the rigor mortis stages. Colder temperatures can slow down rigor mortis significantly. Low temperatures do not stop rigor mortis, however, and as the body warms, rigor accelerates back to its normal timeframe. Conversely, if the decedent had been rigorously active just prior to death, so that his ATP levels were already low, rigor mortis can set much quicker.

> **FUN FACT** – In drownings, rigor mortis is almost instantaneous after death due to the physical exertion the body went through trying to stay above the water.

Even though when rigor mortis is fully set the muscles are "unmovable," it is possible to "break" it. Breaking rigor mortis means you force the muscles to move by brute force. You intentionally break the bond between the actin and myosin. This is not an easy task and takes quite a bit of force, but trying to transport a body in an "L" position off of the death scene is equally daunting.

To break rigor, you must literally force the muscles to move. So, in the case of the body in the "L" position, one person would have to hold the torso to the ground while another would put all of his weight against the legs until the rigor broke, releasing the muscles and allowing the legs to drop to the floor.

Once rigor is broken, the cycle is done for those specific muscles. In the above example, the legs (at the hips) would be out of the rigor mortis cycle and would move freely from that moment on. Rigor does not reset.

This creates another consideration for pathologists determining the PMI. If many of the muscles move freely, does this mean rigor has gone through the entire process and has released naturally, or has someone intervened with the body and broken the rigor? The pathologist would have to assess the entire body to see if rigor is present in any area, like the jaw. Rigor present elsewhere in the body indicates it was broken in the free-moving muscles.

Consider the case study earlier in this book covering Ryan Jenkins. In that case, we know he killed his wife during the night and then transported her the following morning inside their suitcase. He most likely put her into the suitcase before rigor had fully set, meaning he'd still be able to move her arms and legs to make her fit. Once rigor mortis had fully set, she would remain in the fetal position she was found in until it released.

Let's now change the timeline a little and assume that when he wanted to stuff her into the suitcase, rigor mortis had already set. At that point, the only way to fold in her arms and legs so that he could fit her into the suitcase would be if he broke the rigor. She then would be posable again so he could fit her in. After that, rigor would not reset, and her muscles would move freely when authorities removed her from the suitcase, even if the entire rigor cycle was not naturally completed. Police often see broken rigor in bodies that had to be stuffed into a car's trunk for transport.

Rigor often has to be broken at autopsy so the pathologist can gain the access she needs to the body.

As with livor mortis, rigor mortis is also a great way to tell if a body has been moved after death. Let's go back to the example of the dead person stuck in the "L" position. If a body is discovered with its legs in the air, defying gravity, investigators know that someone moved it after rigor mortis set in. Anytime a muscle is frozen in a position that is not natural, that body has been tampered with. Likewise, considering the force required to break rigor, if some of the muscles in a body move freely, while others are still frozen in full rigor mortis, someone has purposely and forcibly interacted with that body.

Algor Mortis

One of the amazing things about the human body is how the different physiological systems work together to maintain homeostasis, which as discussed in the last chapter, is the equilibrium within the body. One of the homeostatic vitals is body temperature, which is kept at approximately 98.6°F/37°C. Immediately at death, the systems keeping homeostasis cease and the body temperature begins to rise or fall to match the ambient temperature. **Algor mortis** is this change in body temperature.

> **TERMS** – Algor mortis is the change in body temperature to match the surrounding environment's temperature.

The common equation used to determine the PMI for algor mortis is: The body loses/gains 1 – 1.5°F/0.5 – 1°C per hour until the ambient temperature is reached. Therefore, if the body was found while the environmental temperature was 70°F, this equation would estimate the body taking approximately 19 hours to cool to that level. However, there are so many variables that greatly affect the rate of body temperature change, these estimates are now widely considered inaccurate and useless.

> **PROCEDURE** – To determine the time of death via algor mortis, the internal temperature of the cadaver needs to be taken. The time of death would be how many hours it would take for the body to reach that temperature from 98.6°F, assuming a 1-1.5°F change per hour. Once the body has reached the ambient temperature, there is no way to determine how long it's been there, as it simply remains at that temperature.

Variables affecting this equation include whether the body was actually at 98.6°F at death, if the body was active prior to death, what type of clothing the body is wearing, whether the body was wet, whether the ambient temperature changed during the time period, whether the body was moved from a climate-controlled environment to a natural one, how the internal body temperature was obtained, etc. There are just too many exceptions to add any validity to the 1 – 1.5°F per hour equation. Because of these variables, algor mortis is not used with any regularity anymore.

There are a couple of methods for obtaining the internal temperature of the body. The easiest and most common is to use a rectal thermometer. This procedure is conducted at the death scene by medical personal or representatives of the coroner's or medical examiner's office. Law enforcement officials on the scene are not authorized to take the cadaver's temperature.

The second method is much more involved, but considered more accurate, but must be done at the morgue. It requires taking the temperature of an internal organ. Obviously, the only way to do this is by cutting into the body and organ so that the thermometer can be inserted. The liver is the typical organ of choice because it is the largest organ of the body and fairly easy to get to.

There are many opponents to this method, not only because it requires specific cuts, but also because it purposely adds artifacts (injuries) to the remains. This technique occurs at the coroner's or medical examiner's morgue, and since most procedures now put the body into the cooler until the next morning, any sort of internal temperature would be negated.

> **ACCURACY** – Algor mortis PMI determinations are rarely done anymore, if ever.

Potassium Release

A much more complicated PMI determination involves evaluating the **vitreous humor**, also known as the ocular fluid, which is simply the eye juice. The vitreous humor is not tears; those are very different. It is the fluid that is within the eyeball itself. The vitreous humor is one of the last things affected by decomposition, and therefore is a desired substrate for biological or toxicological evaluations.

When alive, the cells within the body contain potassium. After death, the potassium is released. Pathologists have determined that if they can ascertain the rate at which the potassium is freed from the cells, they can extrapolate back and figure out how long the release has been occurring in order for that level of potassium to be present. It gets super complicated.

Anyway, to do this, they must take samples of the vitreous humor at several different times (over hours) to figure out the rate of potassium deposits. Once they've figure out the rate, they then take the level of potassium from the first sample and work backwards to figure out how long it would take the potassium to reach that level at that rate of release and call that the time of death.

> PROCEDURE – The potassium release method for determining the PMI is very math-heavy and requires the pathologist to determine the rate of potassium deposits in the vitreous humor by taking several samples. The rate is then used to estimate how long it would take to reach those potassium levels.

This process is so complex, so labor intensive, and so unreliable that it is not a preferred method to determine the time of death.

Stomach Contents

Another method used to help narrow the time-of-death window is examination of the stomach contents. In the Internal Examination chapter, we discussed that the pathologist routinely empties the stomach during the autopsy to inspect the contents. It's as messy as it sounds.

With some variance, the human body takes approximately two to three hours to digest a meal and move it to the small intestine. If the contents are partially digested in the stomach, pathologists know the person died within a couple of hours of his last meal. If the time of the last meal is known, this creates a very small time-of-death window. If there is no information regarding when he last ate, however, the analysis is not as useful. The pathologists would know he died within a couple of hours of eating, but they would not know at what point that would be a couple of hours from. Likewise, if the last meal was known, and if the meal was fully moved from the stomach to the intestines, pathologists would know the deceased was alive at least for a few hours after that meal.

> PROCEDURE – If the time of the last meal is known, examining the stomach contents can greatly narrow the PMI estimate, as most digestion takes two to three hours to move a meal from the stomach to the small intestine.

Entomology

In Chapter 3 we discussed the benefits forensic entomology (the study of insects) brings to an autopsy, both in locating wounds and in toxicological assessments. However, probably the most significant contribution insects provide to death investigations is in PMI estimations. Absent an eyewitness account, forensic entomology can be the most reliable time-of-death window determination, although even here the window is typically days long.

The life cycles of certain insects are well established and consistent; entomologists know how long it takes certain insects to reach the development stage of their life cycle that is found on the body. The entomologists also know that other insects are attracted to the body not because of the body itself, but because of the insects colonizing it, which is what they feed on. So, if these bug-eating insects are present, entomologists know that a greater period of time has passed since death because the colonizing insects needed time to lay eggs and hatch larvae. The natural cycle normally occurs as follows:

- Necrophilous insects, most often flies, eat dead tissue and arrive first to colonize the body.
- Predatory insects, typically beetles, eat larvae and are attracted to the necrophilous insects.
- Omnivorous insects, such as ants and wasps, eat other insects and are attracted to the body by the predatory insects.
- Indigenous species, which are insects and spiders native to that location, eventually use the body to create new homes.

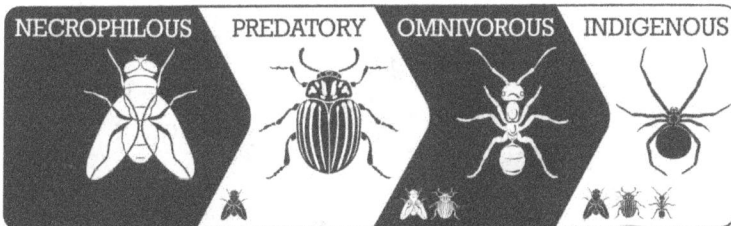

Figure 22: Arrival Order of Insect Types to a Dead Body

The most common necrophilous insect is the blow-fly (the common housefly). They are attracted to a dead body almost immediately to up to twenty-four hours after death. The fly chooses the orifice or wound to colonize and then begins laying eggs inside the body. A normal adult blowfly can lay thousands of eggs. After twenty-four hours, the fly larvae, maggots, hatch from the eggs and immediately start feeding off of the dead flesh. Twenty-four hours later the maggots grow significantly into stage-two larvae. After feeding for another twenty-four hours, the maggots grow into stage-three larvae. After another 126 hours, these large maggots leave the body and grow a hard-shelled cocoon, called a pupa. Officially, they *pupate*. After an additional 146 hours, full-grown blowflies hatch from the pupae, and the cycle begins anew.

> **PROCEDURE – Based off of the blowfly life cycle, entomologists can determine the number of days a body has been dead: 1 day for fresh maggots, 2 days for stage-2 maggots, 3 days for stage-3 maggots, 8.5 days for pupae, and 14.5 days for hatched pupae.**

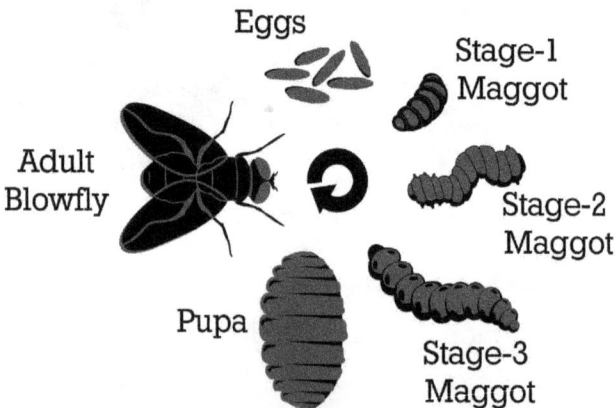

Eggs

Stage-1 Maggot

Adult Blowfly

Stage-2 Maggot

Pupa

Stage-3 Maggot

Figure 23: Life Cycle of a Blowfly

An entomologist trained in all of the specific insects present and the environmental conditions for that area is needed to make a PMI estimate using the arrival of the other types of insects. These time-of-death windows are typically months long.

FUN FACT – Blowfly maggots only eat dead flesh (called necrotic tissue), so in medical practice prior to antibiotics, doctors used to put these maggots into severe wounds so that they could clean out the infected, rotting flesh and treat the injury.

As with all of the other time-of-death determinations, forensic entomology must take several variables into account while making the window estimate. While the life cycles are well documented, factors such as access, temperature, and weather can greatly affect when a blowfly reaches the body, significantly changing when the time-of-death window begins. A body that is indoors, inside the trunk of a car, buried, or otherwise difficult to access will affect when a blowfly can reach the body and how many blowflies will be present to lay eggs. Colder temperatures greatly reduce blowfly activity. A gusty day can allow the blowflies to detect the dead body sooner, while a very windy or rainy day could impede the blowfly's ability to travel to it. All of these factors must be considered by the entomologist.

So, as you can see, there are a variety of methods

that can be used separately or in concert to determine a time-of-death window. However, unless there is an eyewitness account, all of them have variables that affect their reliability, and none of them can bring the window down to the minute. So please view all of the stories with proclamations such as "I'd place the time of death at half past two," with the skepticism they deserve, and consider the real-world complexities when placing time of death in your own writing.

Chapter 7: Writing Your Autopsy

All crime stories are pieced together by the evidence trail that leads the reader toward a satisfying conclusion. An investigator found *that*, which led him *there*, where he found *those*, which directed him towards *them*. However, this concept doesn't have to apply only to police procedurals. Utilizing these connections in any writing genre shows how every step in a character's journey becomes important because it tracks clear progress in the story.

Logic leaps are authorial shortcuts, enabling authors to skip one or more of those links. Unfortunately, while convenient for the writer, logic leaps can frustrate and alienate the reader. If the story progression is choppy or inexplicable, too many readers lose interest in what they're reading.

My purpose in the *Forensics for Fiction* series is to lay out how things work in the real world to hopefully give authors validity in their storytelling. I also hope to provide insight into several potential steps in that story's progression to eliminate the need for logic leaps. As the author, you are the master of your characters' universes. Although something happens a particular way in the real world, your story can bend the rules. Use what works to move your story forward and connects each step. If it's important to you to use toe tags, for example, although this book taught you they're really a thing of the past, then use toe tags. Just make your choices consistent and true to the world you're building.

The Body's Basic Interrogatory Menu

We've gone over the different types of autopsies and learned that there are kinds that have nothing to do with criminal investigations at all. However, every single autopsy has one rudimentary thing in common: they all require a body.

The specifics of that death are essential to you and your writing, even if your characters don't have the full picture themselves. That is why I put together this basic interrogatory menu; to help you get a grasp on the body's importance so that you can easily place it in your book.

- WHO
  - This is the <u>identity of the remains</u>. Who is your body? Is the identity obvious or mysterious?
  - Remember, there are only three ways to positively identify a body:
    - Fingerprints – Requires antemortem prints for comparison.
    - Odontology – Requires antemortem dental

records for comparison.
- DNA – Requires antemortem DNA records for comparison.
  - What if this person was from a rural, impoverished community and had none of those antemortem records? Then the pathologist would rely on less conclusive methods, and she would have to annotate it as such.
    - Medical records – Are there doctor visits or X-rays that show previous scars or bone breaks that the pathologist could compare?
    - Tattoos or birth marks?
  - What if this is a transient person in a bus station far from home with no ID? The pathologist might be critical in determining a background and city of origin.

- WHAT
  - What kind of death was it? This is the manner of death. Remember, there are only five categories, but for you, the writer who knows everything, there are really only four:
    - **Natural** – The death was a disease or disorder independent of outside influence.
    - **Accidental** – The death was not anticipated, even though the action may have been inherently risky.
    - **Homicide** – The death was caused by the

actions of another person, illegal or not.

- **Suicide** – The deceased caused his own death, intentionally.
- **Undetermined** – In the writer's worldbuilding, this does not apply. The *characters* may not know the category of death, but the Master of this Universe *must*.

- WHERE
  - This is the <u>location of death</u>. Where was the body found? Is that area of significance to the body? How about to the characters and the story?
  - What if where the body was found was not where it was killed? How was it moved? Why was it moved? By whom? Where is the death location?
  - What if the body is in pieces, located in multiple locations? What if those scattered pieces are not discovered at the same time?

- WHEN
  - When did the body die? This is the <u>postmortem interval</u>, which is important because it requires the coroner or medical examiner to guess at a window of time that the death most probably occurred in. These time-of-death estimates, no matter how many fictional stories say otherwise, are not accurate!

- Livor Mortis – Skin staining by the blood.
  - Full lividity can take up to twelve hours, but is dependent on environmental factors.
- Rigor Mortis – Muscle rigidity.
  - Each stage in the cycle takes eight to twelve hours.
  - The entire cycle takes twenty-four to thirty-six hours, but is dependent on environmental factors.
- Algor Mortis – Body temperature cooling/warming to match ambient temperature.
  - Highly unreliable and very dependent on environmental factors.
  - The general equation estimates that the body changes 1–1.5°F per hour, but so many conditions can change this greatly.
- Potassium Release – Estimating the rate of potassium release from cells to extrapolate how long the potassium has been releasing.
  - Extremely difficult and time consuming procedure that requires many samples at different times.
  - The results are highly unreliable.
- Stomach Contents – Estimates the time of death by examining how digested the

deceased's food is.

- Requires that the deceased ate a meal, and requires the time of that meal to be known.
- Most people require two to three hours for their bodies to move a meal from the stomach to the small intestine.

- Entomology – Analyzing bug activity.
  - Entomologists can accurately tell how long certain bugs have been on the body, but not when they first gained access to it.
  - The blowfly egg hatches in one day. The maggots feed for 7.5 days before forming a pupa. The pupa hatches in six days.

- WHY
  - Why did the body die? This is the <u>cause of death</u>, the events that led to the death.
  - What if there are several events? Does that complicate the final cause? For example, there can be evidence of severe blunt force trauma from a beating as well as strangulation. Or what if the person was in a car accident (intended?), but later poisoned when he survived?
  - What if two pathologists conclude two different causes of death? This does not

normally occur, but for a story could be a significant plot point.

- HOW
  - How did the body die? This is the <u>mechanism of death</u>, the literal physiological reason for the death.
  - What if the mechanism is somehow missed? Does your pathologist incorrectly report some other mechanism? Does she copout with a "cardiac arrest" finding? Does she settle for a diagnosis of exclusion?

Autopsy by Genre

Autopsies can be a vital point in your story. Whether your story is a mystery, a romance, science fiction, or paranormal, the autopsy can provide evidence, strong emotions, or strange unexplained findings that nudge your characters in fascinating directions. That is why this topic relates to so many different authors.

How can you use an autopsy to further your own story? Again, the answer relies on you, but let's go over examples from a variety of genres.

Police Procedural

I think all writers would agree that autopsies fit seamlessly into a police procedural story. We see them in the majority of cop shows on television. In a sense, they are the primal scene for this mystery subgenre.

When writing procedurals, be aware that fans of the subgenre know (or think they know) the rules of engagement. An increased level of detail and complication can add tension and credibility to your plotting and characterization. A solid sense of the postmortem process gives your investigators a charged, significant environment where personal and professional interests collide.

Weigh the amount and depth of granularity your audience expects. Consider clichés you should avoid and make sure the techniques, technology, and terminology are appropriate for the era, context, and region.

As shown in this book, the autopsy is an important step in the investigative process. But what about for other genres? Could autopsies be just as essential?

Cozy Mystery

The delight of the cozy mystery is the triumph of the unassuming, common snoop over the strict, regulated, experienced investigators. The main purpose of most cozy mysteries is providing the reader with a fun story. So how does a technical postmortem procedure fit in with that goal?

For these stories, the autopsy should be on the side of the investigators. It should lead them either in the wrong direction or down a winding road that ends well after the amateur detective's way did. The message with these stories should be that simple logic outdoes technical clamor.

An investigator intent on proving accidental overdose may be stalled by waiting for the toxicology results, while your sleuth is busy observing family members before she proves the victim was strangled. Or perhaps the cause of death was determined to be drowning when the body washed up on-shore, while the killer actually took advantage of the victim's peanut allergy while out at sea.

The options are endless for our detectives to snoop out motives and methods. But the autopsy is a fantastic tool to give them another roadblock.

Thriller

A thriller always involves a race against time. The reader is aware of the countdown clock as it ticks towards doom. The autopsy becomes an essential step, in a story of steps, which leads the protagonist in his race to stop the impending evil.

In this subgenre, writers can use autopsies to start the countdown clock, such as in super-virus stories like *Outbreak* and *Contagion,* or provide signs and markers in the race that leads the protagonist toward the next wrenching confrontation.

Think of the moths inserted in the throats of Buffalo Bill's victims courtesy of Thomas Harris in *Silence of the Lambs,* or the markings on the curator's corpse in the Louvre that gets Dan Brown's *The Da Vinci Code* rolling. A thriller may use only a tiny detail from a body or autopsy, but that element amps the stakes and increases the danger facing the characters.

Likewise, if your protagonist participates directly in the autopsy, his or her legal standing can indicate power, authority, and experience in ways that deepen characterization. Because so many thriller leads come from law enforcement or the intelligence communities, their comfort level (or lack thereof) can unpack their backstory dramatically.

Historical

Historical autopsies afford an author a chance to play with the cultural assumptions of the societies of that era. What scientific advances did they have to live without? Life in other time periods doesn't have to be, and shouldn't be, just living without cars or iPhones.

The same goes for autopsies. How were the autopsies different in this era? Were the procedures less humane without the tools we're accustomed to today? How accurate where the findings when tests like DNA and toxicology weren't around? How rudimentary were the facilities? How could a misdiagnosed cause of death affect the story? How do superstitions or beliefs complicate access to human remains? How does the legal, scientific, and investigative culture of that time change the ways a dead body is processed and interpreted? How does historical religious rule affect whether an autopsy (the "butchering" of a body) can even be considered?

Burial preparation and scientific investigation are as old as opposable thumbs. Humans have been trying to make sense of mortality for their entire existence. The ancient Persians performed "air burials" on towers which allowed corpses to be picked clean by wind and birds. The Greeks believed the liver held the soul, and the brain was an organ of respiration. The Egyptians carefully embalmed and mummified their royal corpses to prepare them for the afterlife. Many civilizations insisted on burying corpses intact to protect the spirit after death. How does the culture you're writing about handle death and its aftermath? How would their beliefs about an afterlife change the information you could extract from a corpse?

Any Jack the Ripper tale hinges on the limitations of postmortem advances of that time. For example, blood that had clotted and been absorbed by her clothing led to the initial assumption Mary Ann Nichols had been killed in a different location. Likewise, while not specifically focused on autopsies, the medical drama *The Knick* focuses on the medical limitations of the early twentieth century.

Don't be afraid to embrace the beliefs of the era and area. Quack medicine and discarded theories (e.g., phrenology, mesmerism, doctrine of humors) allow you to anchor a story in its time realistically and also introduce ironic confusion or error that increases useful suspense and misdirection. The limitations and errors of the era can sometimes be more illuminating than spot-on forensic science because of the way they set the scene and reveal preconceptions.

Paranormal

Paranormal stories open up entirely different worlds. What laws of nature are different in these universes than ours? When does magic or psionics mess with death or the autopsy process? How does medicolegal investigation of a corpse change if death is literally, physically not the end?

Stories dealing with zombies and vampires often detail aspects of death and decomposition, from non-beating hearts, to cold skin, to marbling, to rotted flesh. Knowing your way around a slab may help you create some killer scenes. How do morgue and mortuary procedures affect your undead characters? How can normal decomposition aid in your descriptions and worldbuilding?

Paranormal stories often use suspense structure to amplify tension. Think about the ways that supernaturals and humans interact. Why do a postmortem if a psychic could just chat with the victim to get their side of the story? How would a magical attack show itself in the morgue? How can you determine time of death in a creature that doesn't decompose like organic life forms?

And what about actual supernatural autopsies? How does lycanthropy change the internal organs of the host? If the person is in his changed form, are the organs mutated at death? What does the pathologist find in a vampire or a zombie? How does a body become undead? And when would be the worst time to wake up during your autopsy? If mortality isn't black and white, how do postmortem investigations deal with "degrees" of deadness?

The same also applies to the creatures and kingdoms of different fantasy genres. How does the anatomy of an elf or goblin assist or impede the autopsy conducted by a human pathologist? What anatomical differences are encountered? How does decomposition vary with each species? What clues or misconceptions does the postmortem provide? As you worldbuild, establish the parameters of vital function so you know what to do when your supernatural characters give up the ghost.

Science Fiction

Much like supernatural stories, science fiction tales can bring in the foreign and unknown to the characters and readers alike.

We have all heard tales of the alien autopsy. Dissection and analysis is a common way scientists investigate a different life form. What does that require? How are anatomy, physiology, and decomposition different for the tissues of an alien species? How does radiation mutate humans? How is lividity affected by zero gravity? How would human autopsies apply to alien species or environments? How would bodymods, mutation, or nanotechnology alter details like PMI or entomology? How and where are death and bereavement handled? What does the autopsy find that defies known science or exposes new inventions? How would a future society's records improve the antemortem details necessary to identify the cause, manner, and mechanism of a death? What new tools and technologies improve the process or deepen the information available from a postmortem?

Because science fiction grapples with the effects of science on human civilization, it offers a unique opportunity to test the limits of postmortem processing. Consider the ways legal, religious, and sociological shifts would change the way we access information about a cadaver.

Considerations for Fictional Autopsies

No matter what your genre, there are several considerations to ponder when writing an autopsy. This book covers several technicalities concerning the autopsy, such as how it is done and what it is for, but how do you put your characters in the thick of it? What's it like to be *in* the room? I want to discuss several key concerns to drive home the *experience* of conducting autopsies.

Spatial Awareness

Once you get into the morgue, everyone there has a purpose. They are either prepping the body, conducting their specialty, or assisting the pathologist. Typically the morgue is laid out in stations so that multiple autopsies can be performed at once. A pathologist only works on one body at a time, so if multiple stations are used, multiple pathologists must be available. Each station has a sink that the gurney can roll up to, as well as overhead lights, scales, and sterilized equipment and containers ready for use. Some stations have their own X-ray light boxes, but I've been in some morgues where there is one large light box for the entire room. While I've heard of morgues that do, I've never been in one that has a viewing area, where next of kin or visitors can watch the proceedings behind a window.

Remember, although morbid, this is still a place of medical procedures. Everything is metallic and sterile. There are waste containers for sharps and contaminated wastes, as well as normal receptacles. X-rays and initial photographs normally occur in a separate room within the morgue, and the refrigerated room typically opens to the autopsy suite.

Break rooms, the next-of-kin room, and the doctors' offices, while in the same building, are not in the morgue. The next-of-kin room is meant to hold any relatives of the deceased who come to the building. These rooms are specifically decorated to be serene and cozy, often having warm-colored walls and comfortable furniture.

Bloody Mess

In many autopsy adaptations in film, the person conducting the procedure ends up covered in blood. This produces the bizarre myth that every cut made by the pathologist results in a spray across her mask or apron. In reality, this is never the case. Blood spurts because of blood pressure. Once the heart stops, so does the blood pressure, so there is no force to spray the blood. Furthermore, as we learned with lividity, after the first twelve hours, the blood has seeped out of its vessels and has pooled at gravity-dependent parts of the body.

> **PITFALL** – The shocking visual of blood spraying every-where in fictional autopsies is pure make-believe. When the heart stops producing blood pressure, blood no longer sprays.

Glamour Shots

Speaking of bloody messes, although blood doesn't fly around the morgue, another thing many fictional accounts get wrong is the lack of personal protective equipment.

It's easier to tell which actor is which when their

faces aren't covered by masks. However, in real life everyone in the morgue takes PPE very seriously. There is no perfect makeup or fixing of the hair in the morgue.

> **PROCEDURE – Unlike their TV counterparts, forensic specialists respect the importance of PPE when dealing with remains. Safety must outweigh dashing good looks.**

Tick Tock, Doc

The actual time an autopsy takes to perform varies case to case. Whether the body is intact, the number of injuries, the number of specialists required, the extent of the decomposition, and the potential for specialized techniques (such as having to rehydrate a mummified body) can greatly extend the time required to do a full forensic autopsy. That said, should all factors be more or less normal for a case, the average autopsy procedure takes approximately two to four hours. Please keep in mind, as I've mentioned throughout this book, however, that the autopsy is not considered complete until the pathologist publishes the autopsy report. That report must wait for all laboratory analyses to be done, which, especially in the case of toxicology, could take months.

Come to Odor

One popular belief of morgues is actually true: Dead

bodies stink. Decomposition smells rank, pungent, and all-around unpleasant. It's difficult to describe, because nothing quite smells like human decomposition.

Keep in mind, though, that most of the smell is due to the waste gases from the bacteria during putrefaction. Meaning, the smell gets more intense as decomposition progresses, as more gas is collected. So if a body is found and refrigerated within the first twenty-four-hours or so after death, with a few exceptions, the smell really won't be that bad. Not enough gas has accumulated, and after it is released by cutting into the body, it dissipates rather quickly.

However, not to gloss over every circumstance, please believe me when I say there are some cases of extreme, pungent, tear-inducing stench. But this brings me to another myth of the morgue, one that I've seen done during actual autopsies: The practice of placing Vicks or some other type of odorous rub under the nose does not help at all.

Believe it or not, no matter what situation you're facing, if you allow your body five to ten minutes to adjust, you can forget you're smelling most every-thing. Your body will acclimate to the smell, which is how people can work on farms, in sewage plants...and in morgues. Just allow yourself to get used to the smell and you'll eventually forget about it.

FUN FACT: Decomposition odors are not your friends! Just because you acclimate to the aromas so <u>you</u> no longer smell them does not mean that they've gone away. They will get into your clothes and hair, and unless washed off vigorously and thoroughly, may bring great discomfort to fellow customers when you go out to lunch.

What happens when a menthol rub is applied beneath the nostrils is you are continually and diligently stimulating your olfactory system: You're reminding yourself to smell. And no amount of Vicks or anything else will be able to mask the decomposition odor. You're just making sure you never acclimate so you smell it during the entire procedure, just with a menthol overlay.

PITFALL – The myth of putting Vicks under your nostrils to cover the smell of the body doesn't work. It only gives you a decomposition-scented Vicks aroma.

Bug Out

Many people get grossed out at the thought of maggots on the body. Let's remember how many ways we've discussed that they actually assist in the autopsy. They don't bite and they don't swarm. They are just babies trying to eat dead flesh. They are easily removed from the body or saved for the forensic entomologist.

Once a body is put into refrigeration, the maggots'

biological functions slow down just as the bacteria's do in decomposition. The maggots actually enter a state of hibernation. They do not continue to eat the remains, nor are they able to cross over to other gurneys and contaminate other remains. They wouldn't be able to travel like that normally, but cooled down, they are not going to move at all. They are just harmless, curled up, sleepy stowaways in the autopsy process.

> **PROCEDURE –** Maggots are a pathologist's friend. They may seem like "creepy crawlies," but in a postmortem setting they aid in finding injuries, providing toxicology results, and estimating time-of-death windows.

Secret Identity

The names *John Doe* and *Jane Doe* are given to unidentified remains in the US and Canada. This practice was originated in England where the fictitious names *John Doe* and *Richard Roe* were used to mask the true identities of participants in certain legal proceedings. Although current English laws have made this tradition obsolete, the practice of using the name *John Doe* as a placeholder for a true name continued in the US.

Today, instead of being used to mask an identity, the names *John Doe* and *Jane Doe* are given to persons whose identities are truly unknown. However, although a corpse is still routinely called a John Doe during the autopsy procedure, most offices now require that all official forms (from autopsy reports to death certificates) use "Unknown" for the recorded name.

PROCEDURE – A John Doe is any unidentified corpse in the morgue. However, on the autopsy report, the pathologist lists the name as "unknown."

No Body is Nobody

What happens if a corpse cannot be identified, if the next of kin cannot be located, or even if they are, the body remains unclaimed? Each of these scenarios are actually the same problem – there are no next of kin to release the body to.

As far as the autopsy is concerned, nothing changes. The remains go through the entire process just like every other body. At the end of the procedure, the pathologist still releases the remains to the mortician. It is the mortician's responsibility to release the body to the next of kin's chosen funeral home.

In situations where the body cannot be released, because either no next of kin is located (as in the cases where the body is not identified, or, for example, for a transient, homeless person), or the next of kin refuses to accept the responsibility and abandons the remains, the mortician has specific rules to follow. These rules are normally established either by the local county administration or at the state level.

Some counties require the local government to buy a burial plot and bury the remains. Other counties choose the often cheaper option of having the remains cremated. In those situations, however, the local government must still purchase space at a cemetery to store the ashes. Unless explicitly provided for in the local or state laws, the ashes or remains may not be stored at the mortuary, as that can be viewed as disrespectful, as well as burdens certified morticians with having to dedicate adequate space to do so every time remains are unclaimed.

> **PROCEDURE –** **State or local laws enacted to address uncollected remains require respectful burials or storage for all deceased persons.**

For complete accuracy, as with so many other varying requirements addressed in this book, it behooves each author to research what the applicable laws are for the area in which each story is set.

Quick References

There's a lot that goes into an autopsy, from the discovery of the body, to who's in charge, to what's done. In the hope of keeping all this information readily accessible to you, I'm providing several charts and lists that encapsulate most of the important data.

Coroner vs Medical Examiner by State

Each state decides whether to have a coroner system, a medical examiner structure, or a combination of both. This chart lists every state (as well as the District of Columbia and Puerto Rico) and its system.

MEDICOLEGAL SYSTEM BY STATE					
AL	Coroner	LA	Coroner	OH	Coroner
AK	Medical Examiner	MA	Medical Examiner	OK	Medical Examiner
AR	Coroner	MD	Medical Examiner	OR	Medical Examiner
AZ	Medical Examiner	ME	Medical Examiner	PA	Coroner & ME
CA	Coroner & ME	MI	Medical Examiner	PR	Medical Examiner
CO	Coroner	MN	Coroner & ME	RI	Medical Examiner
CT	Medical Examiner	MO	Coroner & ME	SC	Coroner
DC	Medical Examiner	MS	Coroner & ME	SD	Coroner
DE	Medical Examiner	MT	Coroner	TN	Coroner & ME
FL	Medical Examiner	NC	Coroner & ME	TX	Coroner & ME
GA	Coroner & ME	ND	Coroner**	UT	Medical Examiner
HI	Coroner & ME	NE	Coroner	VA	Medical Examiner
IA	Medical Examiner	NH	Medical Examiner	VT	Medical Examiner
ID	Coroner	NJ	Medical Examiner	WA	Coroner & ME
IL	Coroner & ME	NM	Medical Examiner	WI	Coroner & ME
IN	Coroner*	NV	Coroner	WV	Coroner & ME
KS	Coroner	NY	Coroner & ME	WY	Coroner
KY	Coroner				

* Indiana has a county coroner system that may hire medical examiners in its districts.

** If a North Dakota county elects a manager, that official takes on the coroner's duties.

Figure 24: Coroner vs Medical Examiner System by State
www.cdc.gov/phlp/publications/topic/coroner.html

Autopsy Specialists

A full autopsy can employ the skills of several professionals. The following chart is provided to help keep track of how many people may be present for the autopsy.

POSTMORTEM PERSONNEL	
AUTOPSY	**PHOTOGRAPHER**: takes pictures at the scene, at intake, and during the autopsy.
	RADIOLOGIST: takes X-rays at intake.
	FORENSIC ODONTOLOGIST: takes castings and X-rays of deceased's teeth and compares them to antemortem dental records to positively ID the remains.
	FORENSIC ANTHROPOLOGIST: evaluates skeletonized remains to determine individual characteristics of the dead person.
	FORENSIC ENTOMOLOGIST: studies insects and their life cycles to create a PMI.
	FORENSIC PATHOLOGIST: performs the forensic autopsy.
	MORGUE TECHNICIAN: assists the pathologist in the morgue during autopsy.
LAB	**TOXICOLOGIST**: runs tox screens on samples to identify drugs and poisons.
	HISTOTECHNOLOGIST / HISTOTECHNICIAN: performs microscopic evaluations of tissue samples from the deceased to identify potential disease.
POST-AUTOPSY	**FORENSIC PSYCHOLOGIST**: performs the psychological autopsy.
	MORTICIAN: embalms the body for burial or facilitates cremation.
	FUNERAL DIRECTOR: releases the body (or ashes) to the next of kin and facilitates burials.

Figure 25: Autopsy Specialists Chart

Decomposition Timeline

The *only* thing certain about a decomposition timeline is that it *cannot* be certain. There are just too many environmental variables that speed up, slow down, or even change the type of decomposition occurring within a body. I guarantee, every available decomposition timeline you can Google has a multitude of exceptions, and should not be taken as anything more than a very basic guideline. In that rudimentary sense, I am providing an overly simplified timeline for you to use as a general guide for your writing.

IMMEDIATELY

- Autolysis.
- Putrefaction.

0 – 24 HOURS

- Algor mortis starts immediately and lasts as long as it takes to reach ambient temperature.

2 – 12 HOURS

- Livor mortis starts staining in about two hours, but doesn't set fully until around twelve hours.

24 – 36 HOURS

- Rigor mortis forms, sets, and releases during this timeframe.

1 – 3 DAYS

- Marbling begins due to putrefaction.
- Swelling is visible in the abdomen and groin.

5 – 9 DAYS

- Face swelling is visible and causes the tongue to protrude and the eyes to bulge.
- Skin slippage.
- If in wet environments, skin slippage allows saponification to start.

2 WEEKS

- Stomach contents liquefy and are forced out of the orifices, including nose and mouth.
- Organs liquefy and are forced out of the orifices, including nose and mouth.

3 – 4 WEEKS

- Skin blackens.
- Swelling is extreme over the entire body.
- Visual ID is impossible.

2 – 36 MONTHS

- The amount of time it takes a body to mummify depends solely on how dry/arid the area is. The faster the body dries out, the faster it is preserved in mummification.

1.5 – 10 YEARS

- Skeletonization depends on temperature, whether the body is protected and/or buried, and how much animal activity affected the body.

Time-of-Death Estimates

The postmortem interval is one of the most important functions of a pathologist, although it all comes down to just an educated guess. The following list shows all of the different time-of-death estimation techniques and how wide a time window each provides. Remember, without witnesses, a PMI is several hours to months long.

WITNESS WINDOW

- Eyewitness or video capture of the event gives an exact time of death.
- Eyewitness accounts or video of the last time the

decedent was seen alive and the time the decedent was found dead gives a definite time-of-death window.

LIVOR MORTIS

- Lividity starts staining at around two hours but is not fully set until around twelve hours, depending on environmental variables.
- If the body is moved before lividity is set, multiple lividity stains are possible on the body.

RIGOR MORTIS

- Twenty-four to thirty-six hour cycle.
- Eight to twelve hours to set.
- Eight to twelve hours in full rigor.
- Eight to twelve hours to release.
- Rigor can be broken before the cycle has completed.

ALGOR MORTIS

- Unreliable equation of 1 – 1.5°F change in body temperature until environmental temperature is reached.

POTASSIUM RELEASE

- Pathologists must first determine the rate of potassium release before they can estimate how long that body has been dead.

STOMACH CONTENTS

- If the time of last known meal is known, stomach contents can provide a two to three hour time-of-death window.

ENTOMOLOGY

- Blowflies lay eggs as soon as they reach the body.
- Maggots hatch from eggs in twenty-four hours (1 day total).
- Maggots grow through stages until they form pupae in 7.5 days (8.5 days total).
- Maggots are in pupae for 6 days before hatching as adult blowflies (14.5 days total).

Closing Thoughts

> "The dead cannot cry out for justice. It is the duty of the living to do so for them."
>
> – *Diplomatic Immunity* by Lois McMaster Bujold

The thought of writing an autopsy may at times seem overwhelming, but I hope the information in this book has made it more accessible. When writing about death, try to answer the following highlights and the scenes should go much easier:

- What are the body's basic interrogatories for your story?
- What type of autopsy do you need, clinical or forensic?

- If forensic, who is in charge of your area, a coroner or medical examiner?
- What level of decomposition has the body reached?
- What specialists are needed at autopsy?
- What are the cause, manner, and mechanism of the death?

You should no longer feel nervous about including death or postmortem processes in your stories. They can add tension or complexity to a story, regardless of genre. Just remember to always make it fit into your world, using your rules. Taking what you need to accentuate your autopsies will lead to writing scenes that are *dead on*!

Glossary

Abdomen – The area on a body located at the lower torso, often called the belly.

Abdominal Cavity – The space inside the lower torso of a body, bordering the diaphragm and groin. This space houses the liver, kidneys, gallbladder, spleen, stomach, small intestine, and large intestine.

Abrasion – An injury on a body where the upper levels of skin are removed, a scrape.

Accidental Death – The manner of death used for deaths that occurred when although there may have been an assumption of risk, the death was not intentional.

Actin – A fiber in skeletal muscles that along with myosin and ATP allows for muscle movement. In decomposition, actin and myosin fuse causing rigor mortis.

Adenosine Triphosphate – ATP. A fuel molecule in skeletal muscles that acts as a lubricant between the actin and myosin fibers, allowing for muscle movement. In decomposition, the absence of ATP causes the actin and myosin to fuse, resulting in rigor mortis.

Adipocere – A gray or white waxy soap found on decomposing bodies in wet environments. Water converts the body's fatty acids into the adipocere through the process of saponification.

Algor Mortis – The gradual change in body temperature starting at death to match the surrounding environment's temperature. Although extremely unreliable, the rate of temperature change is a method used to estimate the time of death.

Anatomy – The science focusing on the human body and its make-up.

Antemortem – Before death.

Anterior – In autopsies, the front side of the body.

Anthropology – The study of human beings. In autopsies, the study of human bones to determine individual characteristics such as age, race, gender, height, and so on.

ATP – Adenosine Triphosphate.

Autolysis – "Self-digestion." A process of decomposition that begins immediately after death where digestive enzymes within the cells, **lysosomes**, are released and begin breaking down the tissues of the body.

<u>Autopsy</u> – The dissection of a human corpse.

<u>Autopsy Needle</u> – A specially curved, industrial strong needle used in autopsies to sew the cuts closed. The needle is hook-like so that when it is pushed into the skin, it naturally curves its direction upward, and therefore back out. Also called a **Hadgedorn needle.**

<u>Autopsy Report</u> – The document published by the pathologist once the autopsy is fully complete. It lists all of the findings of the autopsy, including all injuries and the cause and manner of death. It includes toxicological and histological findings and therefore cannot be signed until those laboratory functions are complete.

<u>Body Block</u> – A rubber brick placed under the corpse to extend and exaggerate the body's natural arch during the internal examination and under the neck to immobilize the head for the skull dissection.

<u>Body Farm</u> – A research area used to study the stages of decomposition under varying environmental conditions.

Bog Body – A preserved corpse with minimal if any decomposition due to a biochemical reaction, similar to pickling, of bodies found in bogs. This preservation is very different than, although often confused with, natural mummification.

Bone Saw – One of two instruments used during an autopsy. One is also called a **rib saw** and the other a **Stryker saw**.

Breastbone – An acceptable synonym for **sternum**.

Cardiac – The Latin term used in medical diagnoses that pertain to the heart.

Cause of Death – The identification of the actions, events, or circumstances that directly led to the person dying.

Cavity – An empty, hollow space.

Cerebral – The Latin term used in medical diagnoses that pertain to the brain.

Clinical Autopsy – A postmortem evaluation that can be limited or denied by the next of kin for the purpose of studying disease. Often the cause of death is an illness known while the person is living. Also called a **Hospital Autopsy**.

Contusion – An injury below the skin that did not break the skin, often a bruise.

Coroner – A county-based elected official responsible for the medicolegal investigations of suspicious deaths.

Cranial – The Latin term used in medical diagnoses that pertain to the skull.

Crowner – An office created in England that was responsible for enforcing the Crown's requirements. Eventually this office became responsible for determining types of deaths, and the name of the office evolved into **coroner**.

Death Scene – The location where a body was discovered.

Decedent – A deceased person.

Declaration of Death – The time a doctor validates that a body is dead.

Decomposition – The natural decaying process of organic material. In humans it starts with autolysis and putrefaction and ends with skeletonization.

Distal – In autopsies, the term used to indicate a location is towards a limb's end (towards the hand or foot).

Embalming – A preservation technique used on human bodies to preserve them and stave off decomposition. Morticians embalm bodies slated for open-casket funerals.

Entomology – The study of insects. In autopsies, the presence of insects can assist in wound location, toxicology screenings, and time-of-death estimations.

Exhumation – The digging up a grave to retrieve a body, often for a **second autopsy**.

Exsanguination – Bleeding to death. Dying because there is not enough blood left in the body to continue bodily functions.

Forensic Autopsy – The postmortem evaluation of a body, ordered by a coroner or medical examiner in cases of unexplained, suspicious, or criminal deaths. The purpose of a forensic autopsy is to determine the cause and manner of death. Also called a **medicolegal autopsy**.

Forensic Pathologist – A doctor specifically trained through residency who performs medicolegal autopsies.

Gurney – A wheeled slab used to transport bodies inside a morgue or mortuary.

Hadgedorn Needle – In autopsies, the **autopsy needle**.

Histology – A microscopic evaluation of tissues to identify any deformity or disease.

Homeostasis – The body's physiology working to keep its internal stability against constantly changing external environmental factors.

Homicide – The manner of death used for deaths caused by another person. This is a medical term and not meant to be used in the criminal sense of legal or illegal.

Hospital Autopsy – An acceptable synonym for **clinical autopsy**.

Incision – For autopsies, a cut on the body made by the pathologist.

Indigenous Species – In entomology, insects and spiders that live in a specific area naturally. This is typically the last category of insect to arrive at a dead body, not to feed, but to use its structure to build a home.

Inferior – In autopsies, the term used to indicate a location is towards the body's feet.

Jane Doe – For autopsies, an identified female body treated just like a **John Doe**.

John Doe – For autopsies, any unidentified male corpse in the morgue. However, most offices require the name on the autopsy report to be filled out by the pathologist as "unknown."

Laceration – A jagged wound. A cut caused by injury.

Lateral – In autopsies, the side of the body.

Lividity – An acceptable synonym for **livor mortis**.

Livor Mortis – An initial stage of decomposition that creates a permanent red to blueish-purple staining of the skin in a dead person caused from the pooling of blood by gravity in that area. Also called **lividity**.

Lysosomes – Enzymes located within the cells that digest and recycle organic material. Instrumental in the decompositional process **autolysis**.

Manner of Death – One of only five broad categories that explains what kind of death occurred. The categories are: Natural, Accidental, Homicide, Suicide, and Undetermined.

Marbling – An artifact of decomposition where the veins and arteries of a dead person turn black due to the progression of putrefaction.

ME – A medical examiner.

Mechanism of Death – The literal physiological failure that resulted in death.

Medial – In autopsies, the center line of the body.

Medical Examiner – Hired board-certified forensic pathologists responsible for the medicolegal investigations of suspicious deaths limited to a geographical area.

Medicolegal – An area of science, often forensics, where medicine, law, and law enforcement overlap.

Medicolegal Autopsy – An acceptable synonym for **forensic autopsy.**

Membrane – In anatomy, a thin layer of tissue that lines an internal organ.

Morgue – The facility that houses dead bodies and where autopsies are conducted.

Mortician – A certified professional that receives bodies after their autopsies. The mortician prepares the remains for burial by embalming them, fills out the necessary forms for cremation. Once completed, the mortician releases the body or ashes to the funeral director identified by the next of kin. If the remains are unclaimed, the mortician must work with the local government to bury the body or store the ashes at a cemetery. Many funeral directors are now themselves morticians.

Mortuary – The facility that houses dead bodies and prepares them for burial or cremation.

Mummification – The stage of decomposition in extremely arid environments where the body is completely dried out and decomposition stops. The skin becomes brittle and brown, and the body is preserved.

Myosin – A fiber in skeletal muscles that along with actin and ATP allows for muscle movement. In decomposition, actin and myosin fuse causing rigor mortis.

Natural Death – The manner of death used for deaths that occurred independent of external influences, such as illnesses and biological defects.

Necrophilous Insects – In entomology, insects that colonize corpses. Their larvae eat dead tissue. These insects are first to arrive at a dead body.

Necropsy – The dissection of an animal corpse.

Necrotic Tissue – Dead flesh.

Next of Kin – A dead person's relatives deemed responsible for the remains.

Ocular Fluid – An acceptable synonym for **vitreous humor.**

Odontology – The scientific study of teeth and their development and decay. One of three scientifically accepted methods to positively identify remains during autopsy.

Omnivorous Insects – In entomology, the insect-eating insects that are attracted to a dead body by the full-grown insects (necrophilous and predatory) already there.

Organ – In anatomy, a mass of similar tissues with the same origin and structure, that work together within the body to carry out a function.

Osteons – Microscopic growths within a bone's structure that continue to produce over a person's lifetime, even after the bone has finished growing. Forensic anthropologist can use osteons to assist in age estimations.

Pathologist – The doctor who performs autopsies.

Perimortem – At the time of death.

Personal Effects – Privately owned items including wallets, jewelry, clothing, and more, found on a body when it is delivered to the morgue. The items are released to the **next of kin.**

Personal Protective Equipment – PPE. A variety of outer layer disposable clothing intended to create a barrier between potential pathogens and the person working with or around the body. Appropriate PPE can be any or all of the following: latex gloves, shoe booties, sleeves, goggles, aprons, masks, and full biohazard suits.

Physiology – The study of the different body functions and the systems used to carry out those functions.

PMI – Postmortem Interval.

Posterior – In autopsies, the back side of the body.

Postmortem – After death. Also, another way to say **autopsy.**

Postmortem Interval – PMI. Another way to say **time-of-death** estimation.

PPE – Personal Protective Equipment.

Predatory Insects – In entomology, the insects attracted to a dead body by the larvae of the necrophilous insects, upon which they feed.

Proximal – In autopsies, the term used to indicate a location is towards a limb's beginning (towards the torso).

Psychological Autopsy – A medical health evaluation of a deceased person by a forensic psychologist in order to determine the mental state leading up to the death to help identify a manner of death in undetermined cases.

Pulmonary – The Latin term used in medical diagnoses that pertain to the lungs.

Pupa – A hard cocoon used by insects in which they change from their larvae stage into their adult forms.

Putrefaction – A process of decomposition that begins immediately after death where the bacteria instrumental in the human digestion process begin consuming the body itself.

Radiograph – A picture of the inside of a body using X-rays.

Radiology – The science of using radiation for medical purposes, including the use of X-rays for internal imaging.

Renal – The Latin term used in medical diagnoses that pertain to the kidneys.

Rib Cutters – Pruning shears used in a medical setting during autopsy to cut each of the ribs for breastbone removal. This gives the pathologist access to the organs in the thoracic cavity. Rib cutters are used instead of the rib saw.

Rib Saw – A saw used at autopsy to cut through the cartilage of the ribs to remove the breastbone. This gives the pathologist access to the organs in the thoracic cavity. Also called a **bone saw**.

Rigor Mortis – A temporary initial stage of decomposition in which the muscles stiffen to the point that they will not move. Also simply called rigor.

Rule of 8s – An overly simple time-of-death estimation applied to rigor mortis, stating the first eight hours after death, rigor is setting, the next eight hours, rigor is fully set, and the final eight hours, rigor releases. However, due to rigor's susceptibility to environmental changes, and that the full cycle can take as long as thirty-six hours, this estimation is deemed too unreliable.

Saponification – A chemical reaction in which water converts a fat into a soap. In decomposition, saponification occurs in wet environments. The water converts the body's fatty acids into the soap called **adipocere**.

Scalpel – A specific straight knife used in medical procedures and autopsies to cut into tissue.

Second Autopsy – An additional dissection of the body, after an autopsy has already been conducted by a different pathologist.

Skeleton – All of the bones of the body, working together to form the framework of the body.

Skeletonization – The final stage of decomposition in which all of the body's soft tissue has decayed away and all that is left are the bones.

Skin Slippage – An artifact of decomposition caused by the gas stretching the body to the point that the epidermis starts to blister and detach from the rest of the body.

Skull Cap – The portion of the skull the pathologist cuts off during the head dissection to gain access to the brain.

Sternum – The flat bone that runs down the center of the chest and connects all of the ribs. Also called the breastbone.

Stryker Saw – A specialized bone saw a pathologist uses to cut into the skull. The blade is not sharp, but vibrates at extreme rates.

Suspicious Death – A death in which the circumstances suggest it's unnatural, unattended (outside a doctor's care), unusual, sudden, unexplained, or from a violent act. Suspicious deaths require a **forensic autopsy.**

Suicide – The manner of death used for deaths intentionally brought on by the decedents themselves.

Superior – In autopsies, the term used to indicate a location is towards the body's head.

Thoracic Cavity – The space inside the upper torso of a body, below the rib cage, between the neck and diaphragm. This space contains the heart and lungs.

Thorax – The area of a body located at the upper torso, often called the chest.

Time of Death – A time-window estimation, made by the pathologist during the autopsy, approximating the probable time the body actually died.

Tissue – In anatomy, a mass of similar cells with the same origin and structure, that work together within the body to carry out a function.

Toe Tag – A card with identification data tied to the toe of a corpse in morgues.

Tox Screening – Toxicology tests done at the lab on

tissue and fluid samples collected at autopsy. A normal tox screening only tests for the most common drugs and poisons, although most any toxin can be tested for if requested.

Toxicology – The science of drugs and poisons.

Triage – In morgues, the process of sorting corpses in mass casualty situations at intake to guard against confusion and comingling.

Undetermined Death – The manner of death used for deaths that cannot be adequately placed in any of the other manner of death categories.

Vitreous Humor – The thick liquid that makes up the eyeball. It is one of the last areas of the body affected by decomposition. Also called **ocular fluid.**

X-Ray – An electromagnetic radiation that can capture internal images of bodies and print them on a **radiograph**. Also, another name for the radiograph itself.

Y-Incision – The cut a pathologist makes on a corpse to gain access to the organs of the thoracic and abdominal cavities. Two cuts start at opposite shoulders and meet at the bottom of the sternum. A third cut goes from the sternum straight down to the groin. The three cuts together form a letter "Y".

Bibliography

- *Criminalistics: An Introduction to Forensic Science (10th Edition)* by Richard Saferstein (January 13, 2010)
- *Forensic Pathology (2nd Edition)* by Vincent J. DiMaio and Dominick DiMaio (June 28, 2001)
- *Henry Lee's Crime Scene Handbook* by Henry C. Lee and Timothy Palmbach (July 25, 2001)
- *Human Anatomy (5th Edition)* by Kenneth Saladin (Jan 12, 2016)
- *Spitz and Fisher's Medicolegal Investigation of Death: Guidelines for the Application of Pathology to Crime Investigation (4th Edition)* by Werner Spitz (December 21, 2005)
- Stahl, William J. *Encyclopedia of Law Enforcement*, s.v. "Coroner and Medical Examiner Systems." London: Sage Publications, 2005. Pages 98-101.

Index

A

Abdominal Cavity, 72, 81, 82,
    84, 85, 86, 87, 175
Accidental Death, 20, 21, 22, 25,
    147, 175
Actin, 130, 131, 132, 133, 175
Adipocere, 118, 119, 176
Algor Mortis, 136, 137, 138, 149,
    169, 171, 176
Allitt, Beverley (Case Study),
    101, 102, 103, 104, 105, 106,
    107, 108, 109, 110
Anal cavity, 87
Antemortem, 32, 33, 41, 64, 126,
    146, 147, 176
Anterior, 55, 76, 176
Anthony, Casey (Case), 22, 24,
    34
Anthony, Caylee, 22, 34
Anthropology, 54, 65, 176
Appendix, 87
ATP, 130, 131, 133, 175, 176
Autolysis, 113, 114, 168, 176
Autopsy Chart, 68, 69
Autopsy Needle, 94, 95, 177
Autopsy Report, 22, 24, 25, 26,
    41, 42, 53, 70, 96, 99, 161,
    165, 177

B

Bacteria, 114, 115, 120, 121, 162
Basic Interrogatories, 26, 28,
    146
Bass, William, 112
Bile, 77, 83, 96
Blanching, 127, 128
Blood, 34, 77, 78, 82, 96, 115,
    126, 127, 128, 130, 149, 160
Body Bag, 59, 61, 62, 63, 68
Body Block, 71, 89, 177
Body Farms, 112, 122, 177
Body's Point of View, 55
Bog Bodies, 120, 121, 178
Bone Dust, 91
Bone Saw, 75, 90, 91, 178
Bowels, 86, 87
Brain, 77, 88, 89, 92, 93, 94, 95
Brainstem, 92
Breastbone, 73, 75, 76, 77, 94,
    178
Bureau of Indian Affairs, 13
Burial Permit, 43

C

Cause of Death, 5, 8, 9, 12, 13,
    18, 19, 24, 25, 26, 27, 28, 34,
    35, 36, 37, 41, 42, 99, 150, 178
Cecum, 87
Cerebellum, 92
Cerebrum, 93
Clinical Autopsy, 17, 35, 36, 37,
    178
Colon, 87
Confirmatory Test, 97
Cooler, 59, 61, 117, 159
Coroner, 3, 4, 6, 7, 8, 9, 10, 11,
    12, 13, 14, 16, 17, 18, 36, 37,
    40, 41, 42, 58, 59, 60, 61, 69,
    70, 75, 99, 123, 129, 130, 131,
    137, 148, 167, 179
Cremation, 16, 42, 43, 95, 166
Crowners, 6, 7, 8, 179

D

Death Certificate, 11, 12, 13, 24,
    25, 26, 42, 43, 165
Death Scene, 16, 21, 43, 58, 129,
    133, 137, 179
Declaration of Death, 42, 43, 59,
    179
Decomposition, 2, 30, 33, 59, 65,
    67, 111, 112, 113, 114, 115,
    117, 118, 119, 120, 121, 122,
    125, 126, 127, 130, 131, 138,
    161, 162, 163, 168, 179
Decomposition Timeline, 168
Diagnosis of Exclusion, 27, 28,
    77, 151
Diaphragm, 81
Distal, 56, 179

DNA Analysis, 12, 29, 33, 147
Duodenum, 86

E

Embalming, 5, 16, 95, 119, 180
Entomology, 54, 67, 140, 150,
    163, 172, 180
Esophagus, 84, 116
Evidence, 1, 11, 18, 21, 22, 25,
    40, 68, 69, 70
Exhumation, 40, 180
Exsanguination, 26, 180

F

Facial Reconstruction, 66
Fingerprinting, 29, 30, 31, 32,
    69, 116, 120, 146
Fiore, Jasmine (Case Study), 45,
    46, 47, 48, 49
Foam, 117
Forensic Autopsy, 17, 18, 24,
    25, 28, 34, 35, 36, 37, 39, 41,
    42, 53, 77, 161, 180
Forensic Pathologist, 10, 12, 13,
    18, 22, 23, 180
Forensic Pathology, 2, 54, 71
Forensic Psychologist, 37, 38,
    39
Frontal Lobe, 93
Funeral Home Director, 16, 17,
    43, 96

G

Gallbladder, 72, 83
Garavaglia, Jan, 22, 23, 34
Glands, 77

H

Heart, 72, 78, 79, 126, 160
Histology, 12, 42, 54, 77, 98, 99, 181
Homeostasis, 111, 112, 114, 135, 181
Homicide, 7, 20, 21, 22, 23, 24, 41, 147, 181
Hypoxia, 26

I

Ileum, 86
Indigenous Species, 141, 181
Inferior, 56, 181
Intake, 58, 60, 62, 63, 68, 69

J

Jejunum, 86
Jenkins, Ryan (Case Study), 45, 46, 47, 48, 49, 50, 51, 52, 134

K

Kidneys, 72, 82

L

Large Intestine, 72, 86, 87, 114, 115
Lateral, 55, 75, 182
Liver, 72, 81, 82, 83, 137
Lividity, 127, 128, 129, 130, 149, 171, 182
Livor Mortis, 126, 127, 128, 129, 130, 132, 135, 149, 169, 171, 182
Lungs, 72, 79

Lysosomes, 114, 182

M

Maggots, 142, 143, 150, 163, 164, 172
Major Vessels, 77
Manner of Death, 9, 13, 18, 19, 20, 21, 22, 23, 24, 25, 26, 36, 38, 41, 42, 99, 147, 182
Marbling, 115, 169, 182
Mechanism of Death, 19, 25, 26, 27, 41, 99, 151, 183
Medial, 55, 183
Medical Examiner, 3, 4, 8, 9, 12, 13, 14, 16, 17, 18, 22, 36, 37, 40, 41, 42, 54, 58, 59, 60, 61, 69, 70, 75, 99, 117, 123, 129, 130, 131, 137, 138, 148, 167, 183
Morgue, 16, 17, 30, 37, 53, 57, 59, 60, 61, 69, 96, 117, 137, 138, 159, 162, 183
Mortician, 16, 17, 42, 95, 96, 165, 166, 183
Mortuary, 16, 17, 57, 166, 184
Mummification, 119, 120, 121, 170, 184
Myosin, 130, 131, 132, 133, 184

N

Natural Death, 17, 20, 22, 25, 36, 147, 184
Necrophilous Insects, 141, 184
Necrotic Tissue, 143, 184
Next of Kin, 16, 18, 36, 37, 39, 68, 89, 94, 95, 96, 159, 165, 185

O

Occipital Lobe, 93
Odontology, 29, 32, 54, 63, 64, 146, 185
Odor, 113, 162, 163
Omnivorous Insects, 141, 185
Open Casket, 64, 89, 95
Organ Bag, 94, 95
Osteons, 66, 185

P

Parietal Lobe, 93
Pending Manner of Death, 24
Personal Effects, 68, 186
Personal Protective Equipment, 57, 91, 160, 186
Photography, 54, 59, 61, 62, 63, 159
PMI, 123, 124, 125, 126, 129, 130, 132, 134, 138, 139, 140, 143, 148, 170, 186
Positive Identification, 29, 30, 33, 64, 146
Posterior, 55, 68, 186
Postmortem, 15, 16, 40, 41, 120, 126, 186
Postmortem Interval, 123, 124, 125, 126, 129, 130, 132, 134, 138, 139, 140, 143, 148, 170, 186
Potassium Release, 138, 139, 149, 171
PPE, 57, 91, 160, 186
Predatory Insects, 141, 186
Preliminary Test, 97
Proximal, 56, 57, 187

Proximate Causation of the Death, 38
Psychological Autopsy, 17, 37, 38, 39, 187
Putrefaction, 113, 114, 115, 116, 162, 168, 187

R

Radiology, 54, 61, 62, 187
Ramsey, JonBenét (Case), 88
Rectum, 87
Rib Cutters, 75, 188
Rib Saw, 75, 76, 91, 188
Ribs, 73, 74, 75, 76, 94
Rigor Mortis, 130, 131, 132, 133, 134, 135, 149, 169, 171, 188
Rule of 8s, 132, 188

S

Saponification, 118, 169, 188
Scalp, 68, 89, 90, 95
Scalpel, 53, 68, 74, 75, 89, 189
Second Autopsy, 17, 39, 40, 41, 189
SIDS, 28, 41
Skeletonization, 121, 122, 170, 189
Skin Glove, 31
Skin Slippage, 31, 32, 116, 118, 169, 189
Skull, 89, 90, 91, 92, 95
Skull Cap, 92, 95, 189
Skull Notch, 92, 95
Small Intestine, 72, 83, 84, 86, 87, 139, 140, 150
Spitz, Werner, 23, 34
Spleen, 72, 85

Sternum, 73, 189
Stomach, 72, 84, 85, 139, 140, 150
Stomach Contents, 77, 116, 139, 140, 149, 169, 172
Stryker Saw, 90, 91, 189
Sudden Infant Death Syndrome, 28, 41
Suicide, 7, 20, 21, 22, 25, 38, 148, 190
Superior, 55, 57, 190
Suspicious Deaths, 3, 4, 8, 9, 10, 13, 18, 35, 58, 190

T

Tattoos, 30, 68, 147
Temporal Lobe, 93
Thoracic Cavity, 71, 72, 76, 78, 80, 81, 190
Time of Death, 28, 42, 43, 67, 99, 113, 117, 122, 123, 124, 125, 126, 129, 130, 132, 134, 136, 138, 139, 140, 143, 144, 148, 164, 170, 190
Tissue Builder, 32
Toe Tags, 60, 61, 190
Tox Screen, 96, 97, 98, 190

Toxicology, 12, 40, 42, 54, 67, 77, 96, 97, 98, 138, 140, 161, 164, 191

U

Undetermined Death, 20, 21, 22, 23, 25, 38, 148, 191
Urine, 77, 96, 116

V

Visual Identification, 30, 117, 170
Vitreous Humor, 77, 96, 138, 139, 191

W

Witness Window, 124, 125, 170

X

X-rays, 32, 61, 62, 63, 64, 71, 74, 159, 191

Y

Y-incision, 72, 74, 89, 94, 95, 191

About the Author

Geoff Symon is a twenty-year Federal Forensic Investigator and Polygraph Examiner. His participation in high-profile cases includes the attacks on September 11, 2001, the War in Iraq, the Space Shuttle Columbia explosion, the 2002 bombings in Bali and the Chandra Levy investigation, among countless other cases.

He has direct, first-hand experience investigating cases including murder (of all types), suicide, arson, kidnapping, bombings, sexual assault, child exploitation, theft and financial crimes. He has specified and certified training in the collection and preservation of evidence, blood spatter analysis, autopsies and laboratory techniques.

He has taught undergraduate and graduate-level college courses in forensics, including Basic Forensics, Crime Scene Processing and Crimes Against Children at the George Washington University (DC) and Marymount University (MD).

You can find him at GeoffSymon.com, Geoff Symon on Facebook and @geoffsymon on Twitter.

Thanks for spending some time with me exploring forensics. I hope you enjoyed this book and found it helpful in fleshing out the crime/autopsies in your fiction. If so, please consider leaving a review at Amazon.com, Goodreads.com or any other site where you have posting privileges.

Visit forensicsforfiction.com for the latest updates and information about the other books in this series.

Geoff